W9-BVD-972

The Pocket Book of DREAMS

The Pocket Book of DREAMS

Interpreting and Guiding Your Dreamworld

PICTURE CREDIT:
All images from Shutterstock

This edition published in 2021 by Arcturus Publishing Limited
26/27 Bickels Yard, 151–153 Bermondsey Street,
London SE1 3HA

ISBN: 978-1-78950-592-4
AD006654UK

Printed in China

CONTENTS

INTRODUCTION

The information that we acquire in dreams allows us entry into a whole library of creativity. Many people admit to having flashes of inspiration following dreams. It is as though a missing piece of the jigsaw suddenly fits into place, allowing one to see the whole picture and then make sense of a problem.

Dreams can be taken as events in their own right and can be interpreted as such, or they can be an expression of the unconscious creative self and contain a message. This message may be given in an obvious and clear way or it may be given in the language of symbolism.

The potential to use dreams for a variety of purposes is huge. When we begin any journey, we

need to plan our route and to work out the quickest way to arrive at our destination. We can use dreams to help us chart a course that enables us to overcome difficulties with those parts of our personality which prevent us from living life to the full. Dreams often alert us to the fact that there is something that needs to be adjusted or confronted. Once we have identified a problem, we can use lucid dreaming techniques to help us to understand or overcome the difficulty. This is where you are aware that you are dreaming and can therefore control your actions within the dream.

Dreaming can also be used to enlist the help of those parts of ourselves which can give us information that is not necessarily consciously available to us. It is possible, in other words, to access or reprogramme a part of our behaviour through dreams. Being

aware that one is dreaming means that appropriate action can be taken, which is what makes lucid dreaming so powerful. For things you are proud of, you can incubate more actions of the same calibre; for thoughts, feelings, situations and actions you have disliked or which have upset you, you can try dreaming about them and, during the dream, increase your will to do better.

This pocket book of dreams is designed to help you dream better. It begins with tips on getting a good night's sleep, through a guide to relaxation, meditation, herbal remedies, and crystals. It explores the magical treasure trove available in our dreams, and how to achieve lucid dreaming. It shows how to keep a dream journal and request the dreams you want, and reveals the most common themes in dreams.

Finally, an A–Z of dream interpretation provides an alphabetical guide to the meaning of specific images in dreams, such as 'flying' or 'teeth falling out'.

We hope that you will find this pocket book fun, informative, easy to use and helpful in making the most of the many hours that you spend sleeping.

Dream well.

There is a time for many words, and there is also a time for sleep.

Homer, *The Odyssey*

You never know. Maybe when we're dreaming... we're more lucid than when we are awake.

Katherine Angela Yeboah

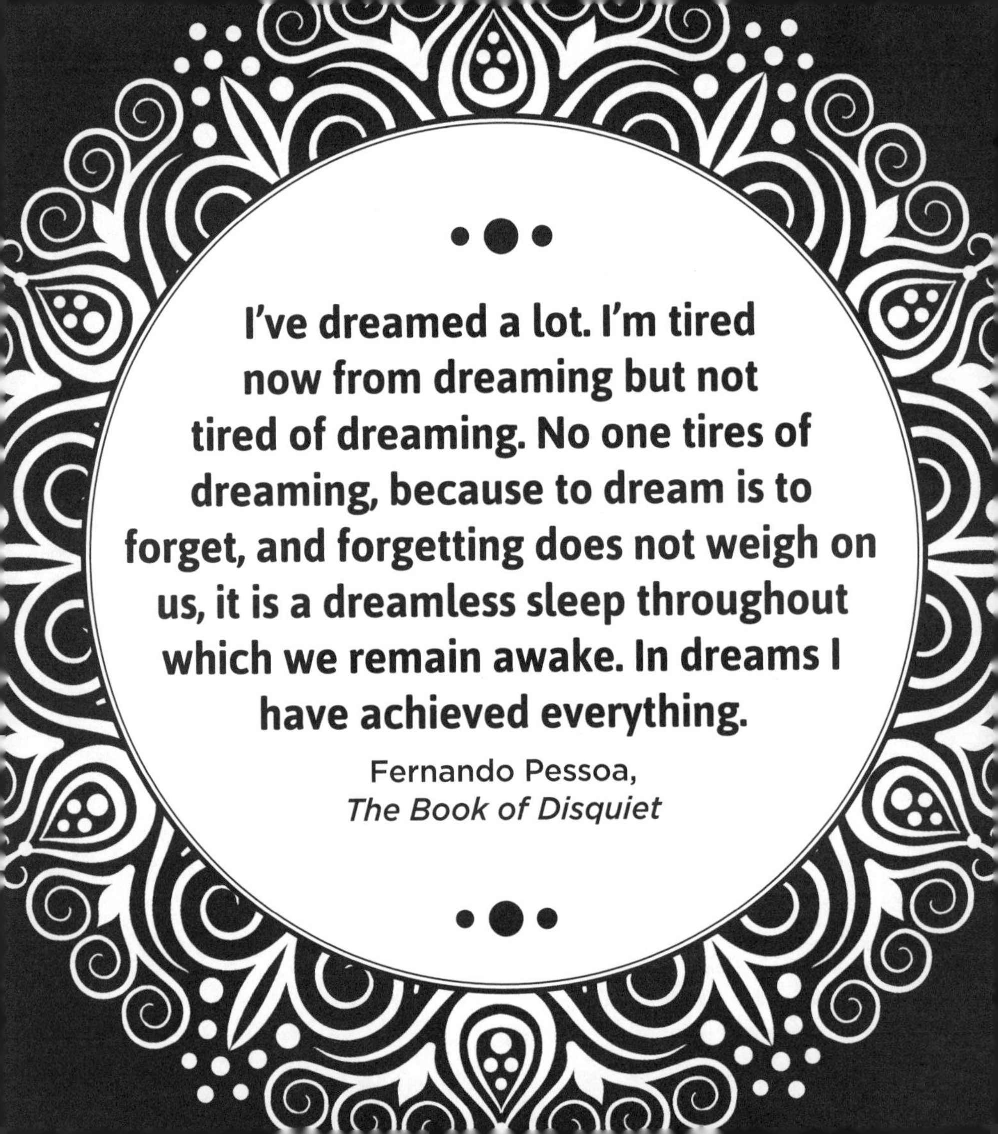
I've dreamed a lot. I'm tired now from dreaming but not tired of dreaming. No one tires of dreaming, because to dream is to forget, and forgetting does not weigh on us, it is a dreamless sleep throughout which we remain awake. In dreams I have achieved everything.
Fernando Pessoa,
The Book of Disquiet

GETTING A
GOOD NIGHT'S
SLEEP

Relaxation

There are many different ways to relax before you go to bed, and you should use whichever method works best for you. Here is a very simple technique that can be done with or without the aid of soothing music, according to preference.

- Find a quiet place where you will not be interrupted.

- Starting with your feet, begin to tighten them as much as is possible, then relax them. Then work progressively up your body, tightening and then relaxing each set of muscles in turn: your calves, then your thighs, your buttocks and so on, until you reach your head.

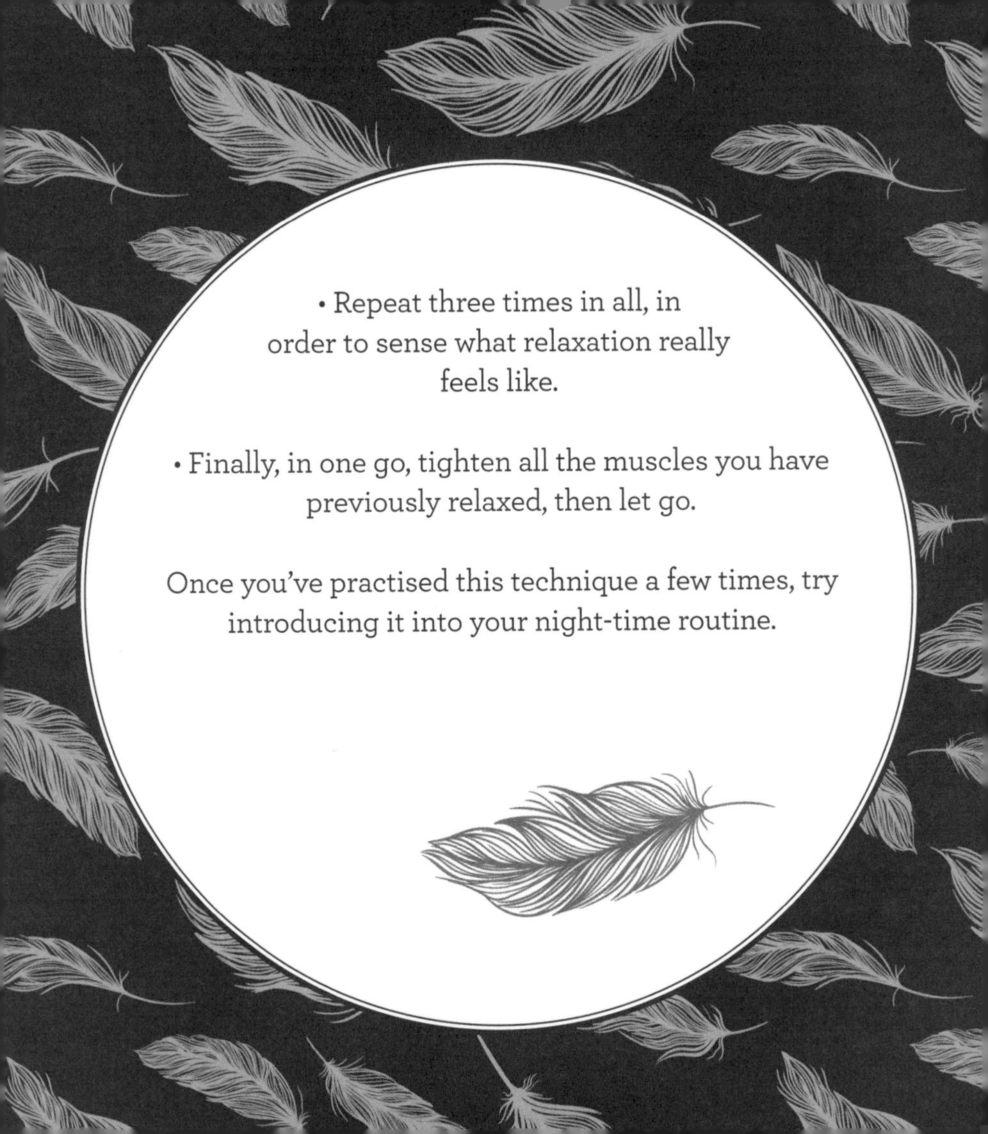

- Repeat three times in all, in order to sense what relaxation really feels like.

- Finally, in one go, tighten all the muscles you have previously relaxed, then let go.

Once you've practised this technique a few times, try introducing it into your night-time routine.

Even a soul submerged in sleep
is hard at work and helps
make something of the world.

Heraclitus, *Fragments*

If you can't sleep, then get up and do something instead of lying there and worrying. It's the worry that gets you, not the loss of sleep.

Dale Carnegie

Each night, when I go to sleep, I die.
And the next morning, when I wake up,
I am reborn.

Mahatma Gandhi

Sleep is God. Go worship.

Jim Butcher, *Death Masks*

MEDITATION

Meditation can be used to help focus the mind and prevent the intrusion of unwanted thoughts at bedtime. It involves three main principles: concentration, contemplation and creative visualization.

- Concentrating on an external object initially, then on an internal image, trains the mind not to be distracted by external sounds or stray ideas – that is, not to go off on a wild goose chase, but to keep the mind on the matter in hand.

- Contemplation enhances this skill, but also improves the ability to remain within your own space, continually observing what appears to be going on without any particular input from you and without trying to affect the outcome. It improves the ability to consciously choose a particular thought or idea for consideration.

- Visualization, on the other hand, helps train you to accept that you can call images to mind or 'make things happen' on an inner level. Having this ability increases the potential for a state of lucidity while dreaming.

Together, these techniques help to stabilize the fleeting images that first appear as one begins to fall asleep and explore the edges of the mind.

THE TOWER MEDITATION

One of the best images to use when meditating before sleep is that of a tower. It can be used to focus the mind, making us ready for information that will help us to live our lives more fully.

- Visualize a tower. Note its shape and structure, but at this point do not spend too much time on the intricacies. Simply note how you approach the tower, including how the entrance appears. Does it open inwards or outwards? Is it strong or flimsy? Is it decorative or plain?

- Now enter the tower and look around. Mentally note whether it is furnished or bare, and attempt to find some stairs; these may lead either up or down. Any obstacles on the stairs may be translated as difficulties which need to be overcome. Each level of the tower can then be explored in turn, noting colours, shapes and anything odd about each stage (often such things will form images in your dreams later).

- When ready, progress to the top of the tower, noting points of interest on the way up. These may require contemplation later on, or perhaps form images in dreams at a later date. When the top is reached, spend some quiet moments contemplating what you have just achieved. Then come back down to each level, noting any changes which have spontaneously occurred. These changes may give you clues as to the types of changes which may be important to you in everyday life. When you get back to the ground floor, take a last look around and come back out into the sunshine, closing the door behind you.

- Finally, walk away from the tower. Let the image fade away and allow yourself to drift gently off to sleep.

You can come back to your tower whenever you like, and next time you visit, you may even discover secret rooms or passages which need further exploration.

Moments before sleep are when she feels most alive, leaping across fragments of the day, bringing each moment into the bed with her like a child with schoolbooks and pencils. The day seems to have no order until these times, which are like a ledger for her, her body full of stories and situations.

Michael Ondaatje, *The English Patient*

Vitamin E, get much sleep, drink much water, travel to a place far away... meditate and teach your heart that this is destiny.

Elizabeth Gilbert, *Eat, Pray, Love*

How about making a personal commitment never to go to sleep without having meditated that day, even if for just one minute?

Rick Hanson, *Buddha's Brain: The Practical Neuroscience of Happiness, Love, and Wisdom*

HERBS

Several herbs are useful in obtaining a good night's sleep and even making our dreams more accessible. These are known as hypnotics or soporifics. Different herbs work for different people; the order given here is alphabetical.

Hops provide a remedy for insomnia, having an effect on the central nervous system. It can be used as an infusion or tincture. However, the herb should not be used if you suffer from depression.

Jamaican dogwood is a fish poison, so should be treated with great care. Also used in cases of insomnia or broken sleep patterns, it is taken as a decoction or a tincture.

Mistletoe soothes and quietens the nervous system, and is used as an infusion or tincture. It is only the young leafy twigs which are used, and not the berries.

Passion flower acts without leaving any kind of a hangover effect, and makes it easy for those who suffer from insomnia on a regular basis to find restful sleep. It is best used internally as an infusion or tincture.

Skullcap has a sedative action par excellence. Working on the central nervous system, it is particularly useful in cases of nervous exhaustion, and is taken as an infusion or tincture.

Valerian, included in many pharmacopoeias as a sedative, is used to manage tension and sleeplessness caused by tension. It can be used as an infusion, tincture or in capsules.

Wild lettuce is invaluable where there is restlessness and excitability, and is both sedative and hypnotic – that is, relaxing and sleep-inducing. Usually taken as an infusion or tincture, it is particularly useful for children.

There are also many nervines (nerve tonics) that have a beneficial effect on the nervous system and may aid sleep. Such relaxants include: *balm, black haw, bugleweed, chamomile, damiana, lady's slipper, lavender, oats, pasque flower, peppermint* and *vervain.*

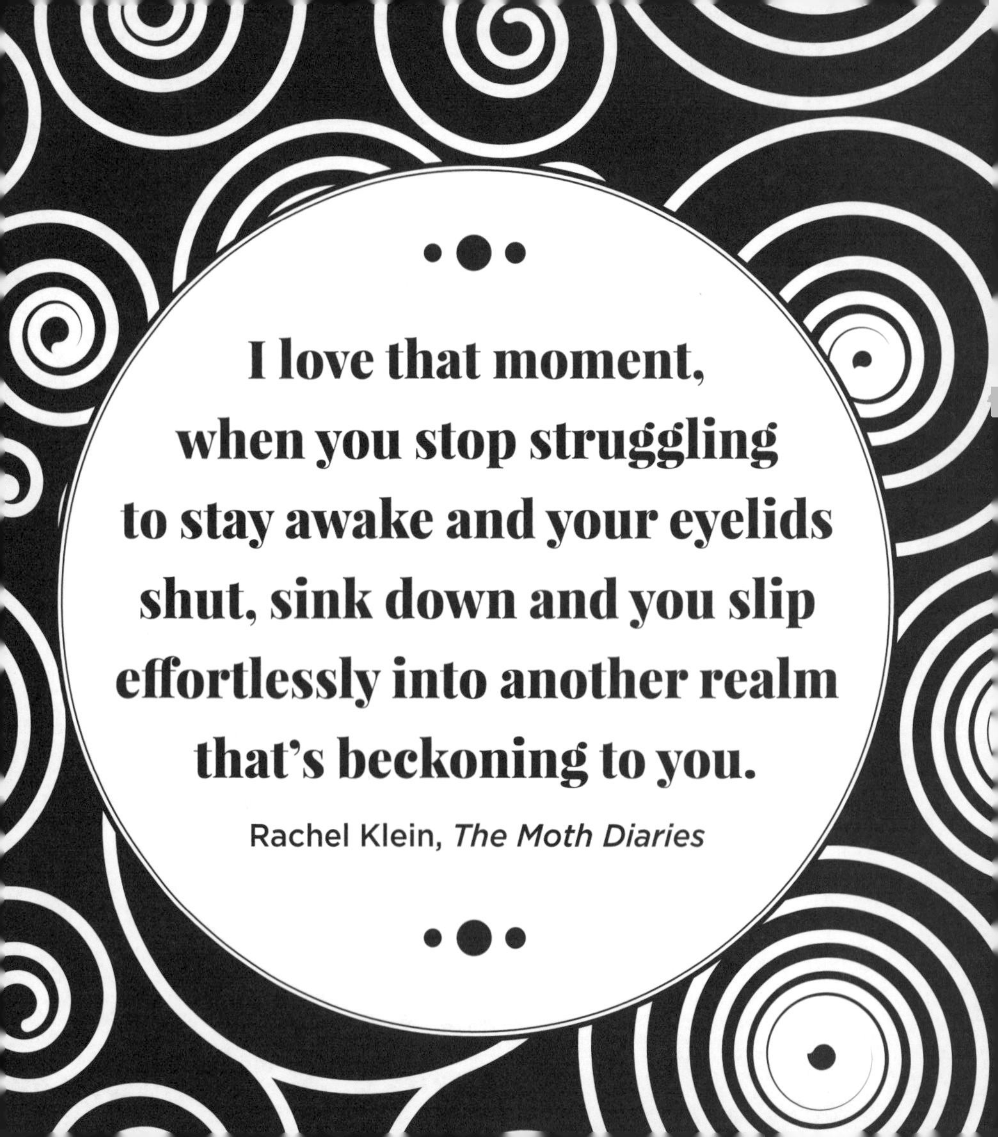
I love that moment,
when you stop struggling
to stay awake and your eyelids
shut, sink down and you slip
effortlessly into another realm
that's beckoning to you.
Rachel Klein, The Moth Diaries

Lie you easy, dream you light,
And sleep you fast for aye;
And luckier may you find the night
Than ever you found the day.

A.E. Housman, *A Shropshire Lad*

CRYSTALS

An integral part of learning and understanding one's inner self, crystals are also aids to sleeping and dreaming. Here are the best ones to try, and their uses.

Beta quartz is said to aid in decoding dreams.

Chinese writing rock is porphyritic with patterns resembling Chinese script. It is good for assisting one into the dream state and directing one's dreams towards the intended subject.

Diaspore gives clarity of dream recall.

Green sapphire encourages the remembering of dreams.

Jade is known as the 'dreamstone', and assists in dream solving and the release of emotions. Place it under your pillow for successful dreaming.

Jasper (red) allows dream recall, as though one were watching a video. It is good for the technique of carrying the dream forward.

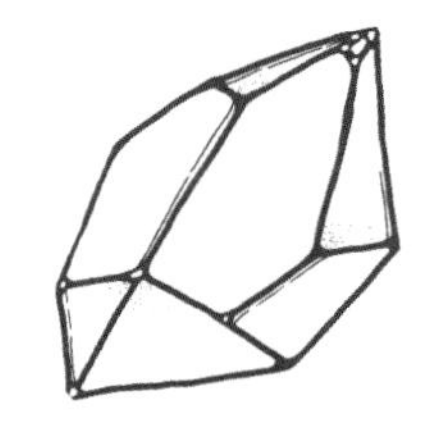

Kyanite calms and clears the mind, and gives good recall and dream-solving.

Lapis gives insights into one's own dreams. It makes a connection with the higher self possible.

Manganosite improves the dream state and helps the memory both during and after the dream.

Opal, the 'happy dream' stone, gives an understanding of the dreamer's potential.

Rhodonite stimulates the vividness of dreams and allows one to 'hold on' to a dream while it is being remembered and recorded.

Ruby protects against distressing dreams.

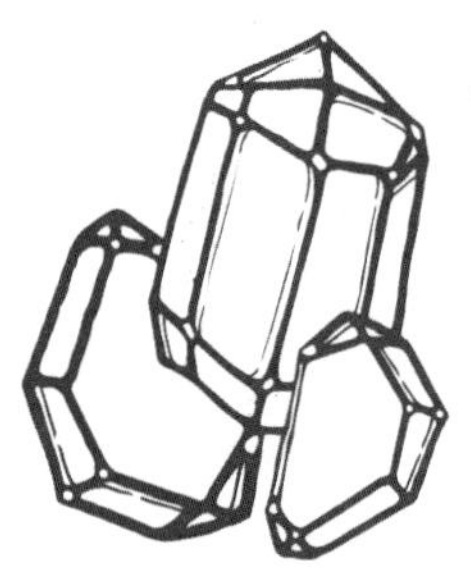

Star garnet helps the dreamer to remember their dreams, particularly those that clear the chaotic state.

Tunnellite can promote creativity and the achievement of one's dreams.

Good night – may you fall asleep in the arms of a dream so beautiful, you'll cry when you awake.

Michael Faudet

If the mind falls asleep, awaken it. Then if it starts wandering, make it quiet. If you reach the state where there is neither sleep nor movement of mind, stay still in that, the natural (real) state.

Ramana Maharshi

TIPS FOR BETTER SLEEP

Here is a quick summary of how to get a good night's sleep.

- Reduce stress as far as you can, and relax. This means doing something which you find relaxing, which may mean an aromatherapy bath using essential oils, having a massage or going for a walk. Reducing stress can consist of reviewing the day, deciding what has been done well, what could have been done better, and what was not done well at all. There is no need to agonize over such things, but simply note them and then let them go. This allows you to leave worries behind, and means that the next day becomes easier to deal with, since it is not cluttered with regrets and difficulties.

- Follow a regular routine as far as bed and waking times are concerned. A routine you keep to without necessarily having to think about it enables your body to slow down into a comfortable idling mode, and helps your mind to relax gradually before sleep. Following a set waking-up routine can also be helpful. For example, do not allow yourself to be awakened by a loud alarm, but use either soft music or a subtle change in light levels to wake you gradually.

- Avoid alcohol or stimulating drinks containing caffeine. Alcohol may relax one initially, but tends to cause wakefulness later during the night. Caffeine stimulates the system, making it more difficult to get to sleep initially, and again lowering the quality of the sleep itself.

- Do not struggle to try to sleep. The frustration of lying in bed tossing and turning can, of itself, prevent sleep and cause anxiety. It is much better to try writing down one's worries and perhaps prioritizing them. Then having done something practical about them, you can put them to one side. Switching to a different activity, such as reading a good book or watching a movie, can help to 'switch off' the brain.

- When you do fall asleep, try to sleep only as much as you need. Your pattern will be totally different from anyone else's, and it is worth experimenting to find the best pattern for you. You may discover, for instance, that you are at your most creative early in the morning, and therefore prefer to preserve this time for yourself, without any interruptions.

- Study your eating habits and consume only foods that are right for your system. Complex carbohydrates are often good, so the idea of a hot milky drink before retiring has some merit. A light meal containing some protein (such as milk, turkey and beans) not too late at night can be sleep-inducing; this is because that particular amino acid is converted into serotonin. Exercise in the late afternoon or early evening is also a good idea.

Any or all of the above techniques can aid and improve your sleep. One way to make up for lost sleep is take a short nap in the afternoon, but you should limit the nap time to 15–20 minutes only. Anything more than that runs the risk of becoming deep sleep. Another idea is to sleep late one morning or go to bed early one night – but not both.

Before you sleep, read something that is exquisite and worth remembering.

Desiderius Erasmus

There's a long, long trail a-winding into the land of my dreams.

Stoddard King, Jr.

Anyone can escape into sleep. We are all geniuses when we dream, the butcher's the poet's equal there.

Emile M. Cioran

Your future depends on your dreams, so go to sleep.

Mesut Barazany

CREATIVE
DREAMING

THE TREASURE TROVE IN OUR DREAMS

The focus of conscious activity is generally geared towards the management of our everyday lives – how we react to circumstances around us, what we think and what we feel. We take in information which must be either used immediately or stored until we can process it and fit it into some kind of pattern. All this activity takes place quite quickly, but at the same time we are receiving many subconscious and subliminal impressions which frequently form the 'stuff that dreams are made of'.

It is this material which often pops up in the dream state in what seems to be a fairly random fashion, but often is not entirely haphazard. It has simply been put together in a different context from the one in which we received it. Dreams tap into a huge database of memory, experience, perception and cultural belief to form new ideas, angles and concepts. They also present us with a way of solving problems that may seem impossible on a conscious level.

Dreams thus perform at least two functions, and interestingly these activities are relevant to the attributes of the two separate halves of the brain. One is the correct sorting and filing of incoming information – activity appropriate to the logical, more verbal side of the brain, and the other is the intuitive, more visually based activity of the right side.

Dreams are the presentation of information – material which is of relevance only to the dreamer – necessary for us to function successfully within the world in which we live. As we become more efficient at opening up to these two potentials, we have more creative energy available to us, and can therefore make better use of our own talents. In dreaming, the limitations that the conscious mind places on the thought processes are removed, and the mind has the freedom to roam wherever it pleases, assembling images at random to suit its own purpose. Free from hindrance, it will create scenarios and situations that challenge rationalization by the logical side of the personality, and yet have a clarity and purpose of their own, if only we are able to 'crack the code'. In looking for explanations, we have to become

more creative and open in the pursuit of knowledge.

Often our dreams will highlight problems or distortions in our waking life, and allow us to readjust them so that we can function better. Conversely, dreams may often distort our carefully constructed beliefs and ideals, forcing us to question many aspects of our daily existence. New experiences, trauma or a reassessment of our own lives can bring to the surface a level of memory which is not normally easily accessible. So a dream is a sort of Pandora's box containing good, bad and indifferent material presented for our scrutiny.

The more we scrutinize the treasure trove provided by our dreams, the more subtle and interesting the explanations become. The simpler, easier and more pertinent the explanations are, the more we can use the knowledge and wisdom that we gain as a tool. Thus, dreams can often be interpreted from more than one perspective in order to be fully understood. Dream interpretation can never be an exact science and must take into account the dreamer's understanding of themselves. No one other than the dreamer can totally understand a dream, however skilled they may be. The dreamer may not be looking for psychological or spiritual interpretation, but simply an easy explanation of the dream. The aim is to recognize that:

- Our unconscious self has information that we need to have brought into conscious knowledge, and therefore the dream is remembered.

- Information is often given in a kind of coded form, where things are sometimes symbolized rather than presented directly.
- Dreams often highlight aspects of ourselves which we do not necessarily wish to deal with, such as sexuality and spirituality.
- The dreamer has a huge store of information with which to create.

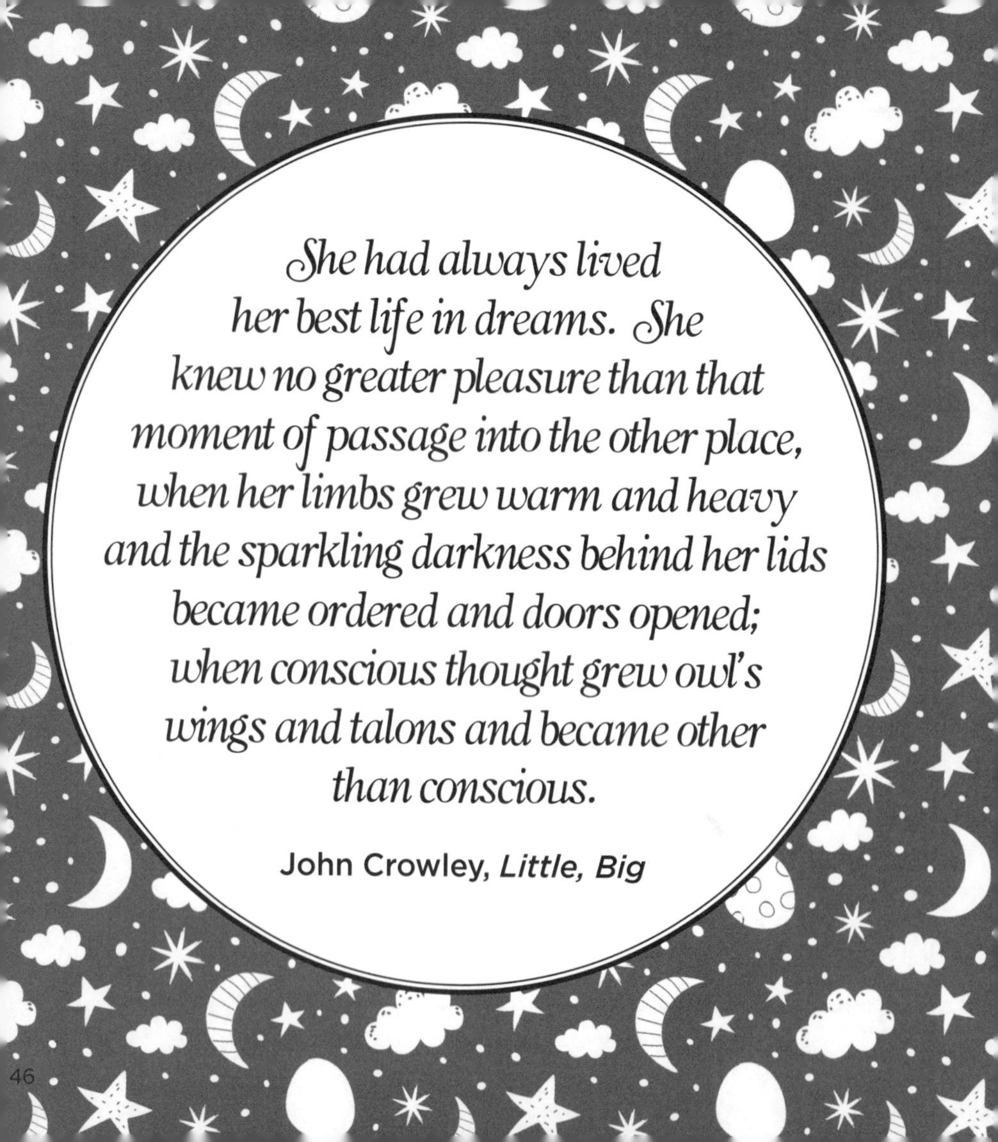

*She had always lived
her best life in dreams. She
knew no greater pleasure than that
moment of passage into the other place,
when her limbs grew warm and heavy
and the sparkling darkness behind her lids
became ordered and doors opened;
when conscious thought grew owl's
wings and talons and became other
than conscious.*

John Crowley, *Little, Big*

All I want is to sleep – to dream. Life is better in dreams.

Christina Westover, *Poisoning Sylvie*

All men, whilst they are awake, are in one common world, but each of them, when he is asleep, is in a world of his own.

Plutarch

TYPES OF DREAMS

It is generally recognized that dreams tend to be of two types: those that the psychologist Carl Jung called 'big' and 'little' dreams. Big dreams are usually easily remembered and the relevance recognized fairly quickly by the dreamer, whereas the significance of lesser dreams may not become apparent until all the themes and dimensions have been explored. Frequently, important and less important dreams can be compared and contrasted by the dreamer. The themes which are first presented in 'big' dreams are often enhanced and better understood by subsequent 'little' dreams. The more proficient the dreamer becomes at recording their dreams, the easier they are remembered.

Another way of categorizing dreams is by dividing them into 'good' and 'bad' dreams. It should be noted, however, that with a greater degree of knowledge, the dreamer can actually change the outcome of a bad dream into a good one.

Sometimes in dreams there is an intensity of emotion which can be extremely frightening. We may be incapable of feeling such an emotion in everyday life, but for some reason can allow ourselves to be terrified in nightmares. It is almost as though we know we can escape from the situation simply by waking up. One of the features of nightmares is feeling stuck in impossible situations or of trying to escape. Often there appears to be no explanation for this until we explore past experiences and anxieties. Being able to disentangle such disturbing images, and treat them in isolation, brings a greater understanding of our doubts and fears.

One of the most frequent dream themes is some form of anxiety. Anxiety dreams – while less intense than nightmares – often allow us to replay, and thus capture, those aspects of our lives which cause us difficulty. Many dreams seem to be about things we are afraid of, but only because they have more impact than others. Disturbing elements in our dreams arise from our memories, stray thoughts or impressions and our own emotions which we deliberately suppress during waking hours. Subliminal worries and problems can be allowed to surface with safety in anxiety dreams. While the images may appear to be the important part of such a dream, it is actually the emotion experienced which needs to be faced and recognized. By doing this, we become better able to handle ordinary, everyday anxieties.

Often by deliberately facing our hidden anxieties, dreams will give us information about what action needs to be taken to enable us to avoid making mistakes. Knowledge of the future may be revealed through hidden anxieties.

Precognitive dreams are an interesting phenomenon. Opinions vary as to whether there are really such things.

Suffice to say that when anxieties are dealt with and further insights gained, the dream will often present the best course of action available and give this information through images. That course of action is then usually chosen by the dreamer, although it may be that the conscious mind does not readily accept the situation.

Magical dreams are also part of the framework of awareness, although there are those who will deny their existence. Dreams are often found to give information in esoteric ways. Number and colour and all of the symbolism contained therein are all a valid part of dream interpretation, and with a little knowledge can create a structure which allows access to what would otherwise be hidden information. Tradition that is based on wisdom, and rituals and ceremonies built around a knowledge of symbolism, are thus accessed. Personal management of the creative side of oneself becomes possible both through dreams, and dreams can act as a monitor for correct behaviour.

STAGES IN SLEEP AND DREAMING

Over the years, a much greater understanding has been gained of the links between sleeping and dreaming. Research into sleep rather than dreaming initially established that the pattern of the brainwaves changed as sleep occurred, and certain common patterns were identified in brain activity during sleep.

Electroencephalogram (EEG) brainwave patterns reveal a kind of progression. In the waking state, the wave activity is low but the frequency is fast. As we relax, the brain produces alpha waves, which in the first stage of sleep then sink into theta waves. In 1953, the pioneer sleep scientist Eugene Aserinsky identified stages in sleep where Rapid Eye Movement (REM) occurred, and in 1957, Rapid Eye Movement was tied in with dreaming. It appeared that REM was some sort of scanning activity.

Alpha brainwaves range from 8–9 or 11–12 cycles per second, and are perceived as a feature of the state of deep meditation practised by trained practitioners of Yoga, Zen and

Sufism – all exponents of the state of 'watchful awareness'.

Beta wave activity happens when there is mental effort, concentration or watchfulness, and at this time the electrical activity of the brain is greatest. It is recorded at frequencies of 13 cycles per second and above, up to about 26 per second. These frequencies can be evoked by anxiety.

Theta brain waves, slower than the waves associated with relaxation, are in the range of 4–7 cycles per second. Oddly, they register during feelings of embarrassment and frustration, but are also linked with creativity and inspiration. Perhaps they are the interface between the physical and the spiritual realms.

Delta brain waves range from 0.5–3 cycles per second, and are connected with deep sleep and a withdrawal from conscious activity. Irregular delta rhythms are very common in the months before and after birth, which is apparently associated with the release of the growth hormone. This ties in with the more esoteric belief that a baby 'dreams' themselves into existence.

Gamma brain waves have a frequency of 27 cycles plus per second, and as yet are not fully investigated nor generally accepted as being distinct from beta waves.

REM sleep was at one time thought to be the only time during which dreams occurred, and it is these dreams which are normally categorized as being worthy of interpretation. They are usually active and realistic, although sometimes somewhat bizarre. We do also dream during Non-Rapid Eye Movement (NREM) times, but the dream content is very different, less discernible, shadowy and more akin to thought forms. It seems that these latter are less easily reported and fade on waking.

The first period of dreaming REM sleep happens about an hour after we have first gone to sleep and into a state of deep relaxation. Unless we are woken immediately after this, we are liable to lose or forget the dream. Oddly, however, we are less easily aroused at this point than at any other. We then travel back up the scale until it seems as though we are almost waking; REM and NREM sleep then alternate four or five times in the night. The longest period of REM sleep occurs just before waking in the morning, and it is these dreams which are remembered most clearly and are most readily available for interpretation.

Physiologically, the brain seems to produce less of two substances called serotonin and noradrenaline during sleep. Both of these substances are involved in the transmission of nerve impulses and messages to the brain, and may be involved in waking activity. We do not know whether sleep is affected by these two substances or vice versa. Deep meditation seems to have the same effect on the body as sleep, although it does appear that psychologically and biologically we do need the escape of the sleep state.

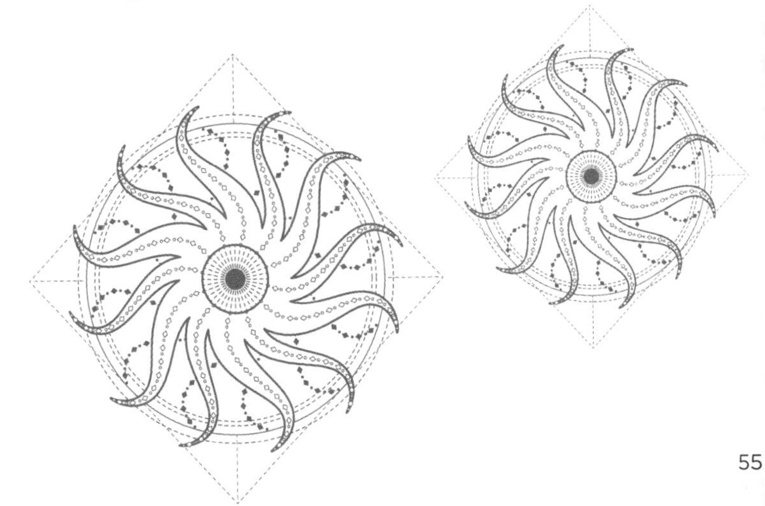

Dreams feel real while we're in them. It's only when we wake up that we realize something was actually strange.

Inception

Dreams are illustrations... from the book your soul is writing about you.

Marsha Norman, *The Fortune Teller*

HYPNAGOGIC AND HYPNOPOMPIC STATES

The hypnagogic and hypnopompic states can be thought of as the entrances to the 'bridge' between waking and sleeping. It is thought that the more an individual's creativity is recognized and developed, the more potential there is both for hypnagogic images and later for 'creative dreaming'.

The rich imagery which is available to us in dreams means that we must learn to make use of two states of awareness. These are of prime importance in the management and understanding of dreams. Many people feel that the states of alertness which occur just before (hypnagogic) and just after (hypnopompic) sleep are akin to – or may even be – creative dreaming. Certainly they are both times in which the material available to the dreaming self is presented for review. In the latter state, one is aware that one is dreaming, but in the former, one is aware that one is not. Some dream interpreters feel that the hypnagogic state particularly is very similar to the creative dreaming one; it is certainly worthwhile comparing them.

In the hustle and bustle of everyday life, it is very easy to lose the images which manifest in dreams. The hypnopompic state occurs between sleeping and waking up, and is one in which we are often able to retain the images of the dream state, to remember the 'great' dreams or anything which we consider to be important. In this state, the images are not necessarily connected with one another, but pop up at random and very quickly disappear. Only if we train ourselves to remember and work with the images do we make use of this state. It is often in this condition that the dreamer hears their name called, and the voice is often that of a relative who is no longer alive. With practice, this can be a time when wishes and desires can be given substance and brought into reality.

The hypnagogic state occurs between being awake and going to sleep. As the untrained dreamer settles into the sleep state, images occur apparently without any particular order. Such images might be of tranquil scenes or beautiful landscapes. Archetypal images representing concepts such as the four elements, animals and spirit faces – familiar or otherwise – can also occur. This is akin to the wide-ranging scanning a graphic artist undertakes when selecting pictures to illustrate a particular theme. It is doubtful that the dreamer necessarily knows or recognizes any of the images shown.

As the dreamer begins to accept more responsibility for their dreams, the images become more pertinent. The more the dreamer becomes open to such images, the quicker their mind responds to the inner images: the images become more meaningful and detailed, tending to appear more rapidly when their validity is accepted. It is sometimes worthwhile to use straightforward dream symbolism to make sense of the figures and shapes which can appear in the hypnagogic state. During the semi-dream state and the fluctuation of awareness of the hypnagogic period, images may be transient but nevertheless offer food for thought and a way of getting rid of the remaining traces of everyday existence (known as the 'day's residue'). This leaves the mind free to deal with the more meaningful images which can then be released through either creative or conventional dreaming. It seems that the mind is more receptive to 'programming' for dreaming in both the hypnagogic and hypnopompic states.

The faculties of clairvoyance (clarity of perception), clairaudience (the hearing of auditory fragments) and precognition (knowledge of a future event) can all become apparent during the hypnagogic period. During this time, images often become very well defined and the individual 'knows' something which was previously unknown or even unknowable.

LUCID DREAMING

An extension of the hypnogogic and hypnopompic states of alertness, in lucid dreaming we know we are dreaming. With training and practice, we can go even further and actually gain an element of control over our dreams. Decisions can be made as to which direction we wish to manipulate our dreams; this can be used to turn a bad dream into a dream with a reasonable or happy ending.

Having become aware that one is dreaming – a kind of 'a-ha' experience – the dream becomes somehow more real. Dream images appear brighter, sharper and more easily accessible, and one is able then to take control. It is important to accept, however, that it is difficult to dream lucidly all the time. Although techniques such as meditation can be developed, they are not always reliable; after having worked several

times in succession, they can suddenly stop working. This is one of the qualities of lucid dreaming – it can manifest a quality of unexpectedness which can be disconcerting. Some believe that parts of dreams can be lucid while other parts are not. So, although one knows that one is dreaming, it also appears that the final decision remains with the dreaming self rather than the conscious self.

Lucid dreams were first recorded as far back as the 5th century AD by Saint Augustine. Slightly later than that, the Tibetans perfected a way of remaining aware throughout the whole process of dreaming, and consequently achieved an understanding of themselves that may be greater than we have today.

It was not until the early 19th century that any sort of scientific explanation was sought; lucid dreaming received much attention when many people were attempting to call up the spirits through the use of

dreams. In the late 1860s, a book entitled *Dreams and How to Guide Them* by Saint Denys documented much of his own research on lucid dreaming. Then, as now, it was important to develop dream recall before becoming aware that one was dreaming.

Technically, lucid dreaming occurs when one becomes aware at some stage in a dream that one is actually dreaming. A simple test of this is to notice that an action or occurrence would not be possible within everyday life, and therefore it indicates that one must be dreaming.

By maintaining a state of alert watchfulness, it is possible to manipulate the dreaming process, possibly from an unwanted negative ending to a positive one. Often the simple realization that we have such a degree of control over what should be an unconscious process is enough to open up all sorts of possibilities in our waking life. It becomes possible to introduce

far more positivity into the management of the circumstances around us than formerly, and also alerts us to the idea that we can actually use the dream state to lay the foundation for things which happen later.

Thus, once we know we can change the outcome of a dream, there is no reason why we cannot change the outcome of our lives; by learning how to manage our dreams, we can enhance our lifestyles. When we become aware of our ability to be creative within the external world, there begins a two-way traffic. It is as though there is a dialogue which goes on between the internal and external self. The two parts of us, rather than being in conflict, begin to co-operate with one another. When this co-operation is consolidated, it should be possible to make things happen in an almost magical way.

The best thing about dreams is that fleeting moment, when you are between asleep and awake, when you don't know the difference between reality and fantasy, when for just that one moment you feel with your entire soul that the dream is reality, and it really happened.

James Arthur Baldwin

All that we see or seem, is but a dream within a dream.

Edgar Allan Poe

All the things one has forgotten scream for help in dreams.

Elias Canetti

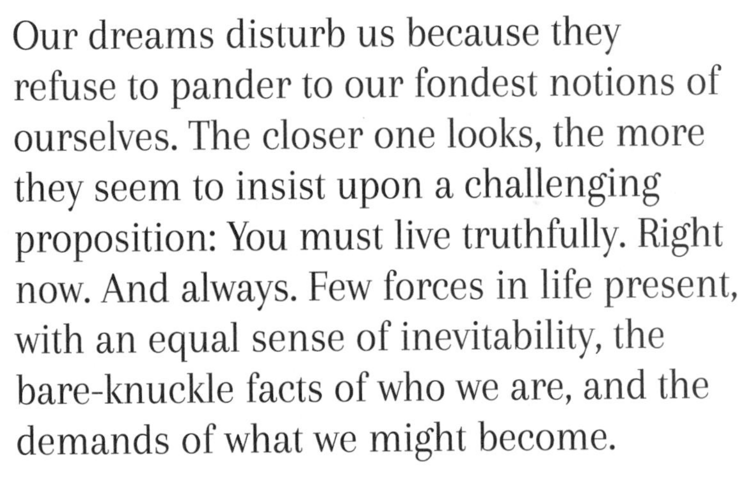

Our dreams disturb us because they refuse to pander to our fondest notions of ourselves. The closer one looks, the more they seem to insist upon a challenging proposition: You must live truthfully. Right now. And always. Few forces in life present, with an equal sense of inevitability, the bare-knuckle facts of who we are, and the demands of what we might become.

Marc Ian Barasch

MANAGING
YOUR
DREAMS

Keeping a Dream Journal

Recording our dreams is a fascinating task, and over time can give us some interesting insights. We may find that we go through a period when most of our dreams seem to be around a particular theme, and once we come to terms with that theme, we can put it to one side.

Keeping a notebook and pencil on the bedside table works well for most people as a method of recording dreams. It is a good idea to write as briefly and succinctly as possible as soon as you wake up. Make a note of your feelings and emotions too, and anything that was odd about the dream. Here's a simple template you could follow:

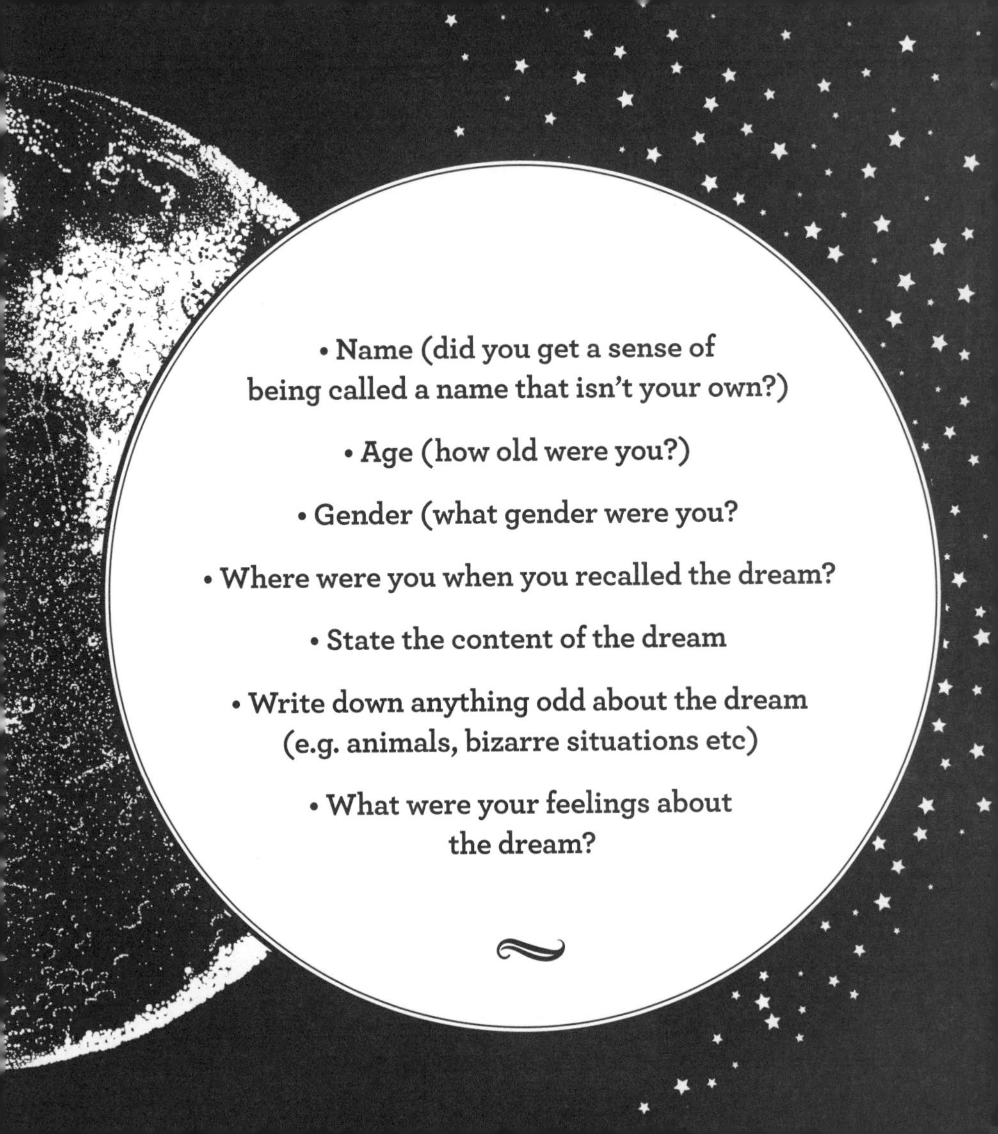

- Name (did you get a sense of being called a name that isn't your own?)
- Age (how old were you?)
- Gender (what gender were you?
- Where were you when you recalled the dream?
- State the content of the dream
- Write down anything odd about the dream (e.g. animals, bizarre situations etc)
- What were your feelings about the dream?

If you wish, you could keep
more extensive records of your dreams.
It can be helpful to record the approximate
time you had the dream, as this will enable you
to pinpoint your most fertile dreaming periods.

If you are just beginning to record your dreams, the
most important thing is not to try too hard. Being
relaxed about the whole thing will give far more
potential for success than getting worked up because
you cannot remember your dream or because you
do not appear to have dreamed at all. The more
you practise, the easier it becomes.

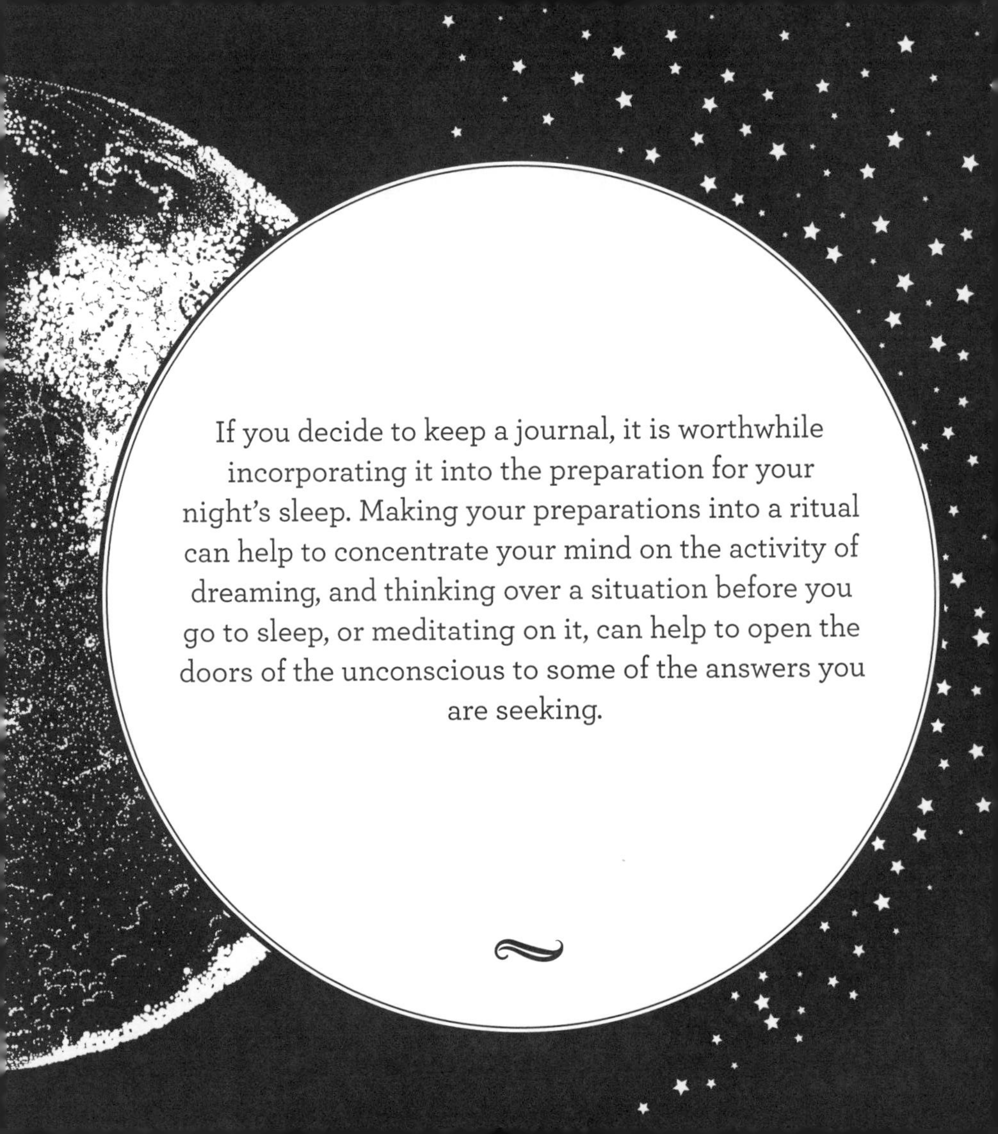

If you decide to keep a journal, it is worthwhile incorporating it into the preparation for your night's sleep. Making your preparations into a ritual can help to concentrate your mind on the activity of dreaming, and thinking over a situation before you go to sleep, or meditating on it, can help to open the doors of the unconscious to some of the answers you are seeking.

REMEMBERING YOUR DREAMS

To be able to remember your dreams, you need to train yourself to do so. Good-quality sleep is the first prerequisite since, while you are learning, you may well be waking yourself up fairly frequently. It is important to get into the habit of a routine conducive to dream recollection.

As a first step, when you wake up in the morning, lie still and try to recall your dream. It does not matter if you can only catch hold of a small fragment. Ask yourself the question, 'What was I dreaming about?' Gradually, with practice, you will remember more and more of your dream. As a reality test, check that you really are awake – take a note of the exact time you wake up, for future reference.

The reason you should lie still is because movement seems to 'chase away' the dream, whereas remaining still helps to 'set' it so that it is more easily recalled. Learning such a habit will also enable you to go back more easily into the dream state.

We know that we dream more prolifically in those periods of Rapid Eye Movement (REM) which take place at approximately 90-minute periods after we have first fallen asleep. If you wish, you can train yourself to wake up at appropriate intervals, firstly by using your alarm clock or phone, and later by simply telling yourself that you will wake up. Under no circumstances allow yourself to be 'shocked' into wakefulness – by very loud music, for example. That is counter-productive because it is most likely to chase away the dream. Use the same technique of lying quite still until you have recalled some aspect of a dream. It does not matter if this process seems difficult at first – it gets easier with practice. Only when you have recalled as much as you can, use your dream journal to record as much detail as you can.

Do remember that often the details of one dream can appear in another one – nothing is too trivial to record. If you have remembered a detail, it has relevance. It is suggested, however, that you practise at weekends – or those days when you are not running to a tight schedule.

He awoke, opened his eye. The room meant very little to him; he was too deeply immersed in the non-being from which he had just come. If he had not the energy to ascertain his position in time and space, he also lacked the desire. ... In utter comfort, utter relaxation he lay absolutely still for a while, and then sank back into the light momentary sleeps that occur after a long, profound one.

Paul Bowles, *The Sheltering Sky*

Dreams are often most profound when they seem the most crazy.

Sigmund Freud

Dreaming is an act of pure imagination, attesting in all men a creative power, which if it were available in waking, would make every man a Dante or Shakespeare.

H.F. Hedge

Dreams are today's answers to tomorrow's questions.

Edgar Cayce

ASKING FOR THE DREAMS YOU WANT

THE NEXT STAGE in managing your dreams is to ask for the dreams you want. The technique given here is of most use when there is a strong, passionate, deeply felt association with the question or request. It works most effectively for those who have already learnt how to recall and record their dreams, because they have already established the lines of communication, but it also works well for those who have learnt to meditate.

The method is very simple. You just need to remember the acronym 'CARDS':

- Clarify the issue.
- Ask the question.
- Repeat it.
- Dream and document it.
- Study the dream.

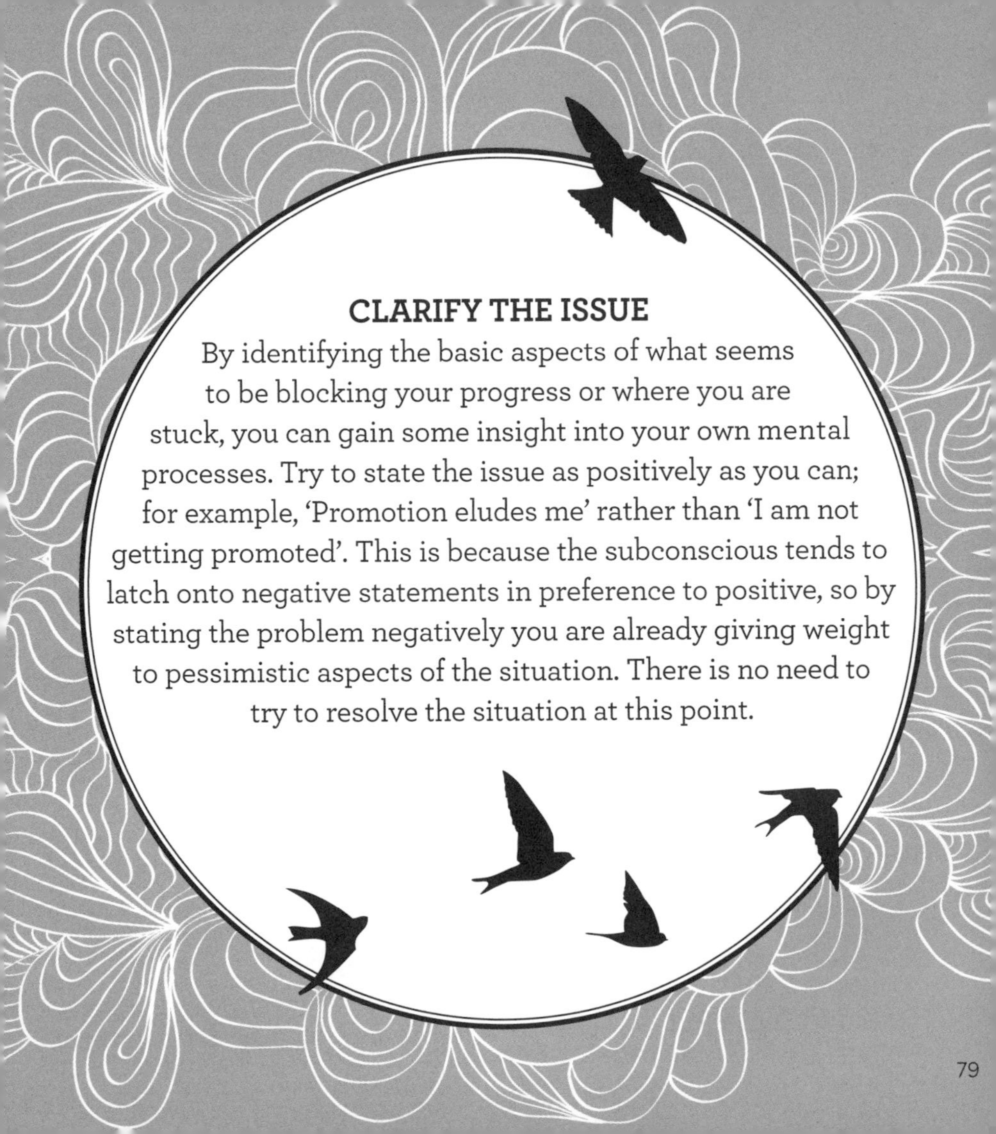

CLARIFY THE ISSUE

By identifying the basic aspects of what seems to be blocking your progress or where you are stuck, you can gain some insight into your own mental processes. Try to state the issue as positively as you can; for example, 'Promotion eludes me' rather than 'I am not getting promoted'. This is because the subconscious tends to latch onto negative statements in preference to positive, so by stating the problem negatively you are already giving weight to pessimistic aspects of the situation. There is no need to try to resolve the situation at this point.

ASK THE QUESTION

Using an old journalistic technique, ask 'Who? What? Where? When? Why?' and sort out in your mind exactly what the relevant question is. For instance, in our example, you might ask:

Who can best help in my search for promotion?

What must I do to be in line for promotion?

Where do the best opportunities lie for me?

When will I be able to use my greater experience?

Why is my expertise not being recognized?

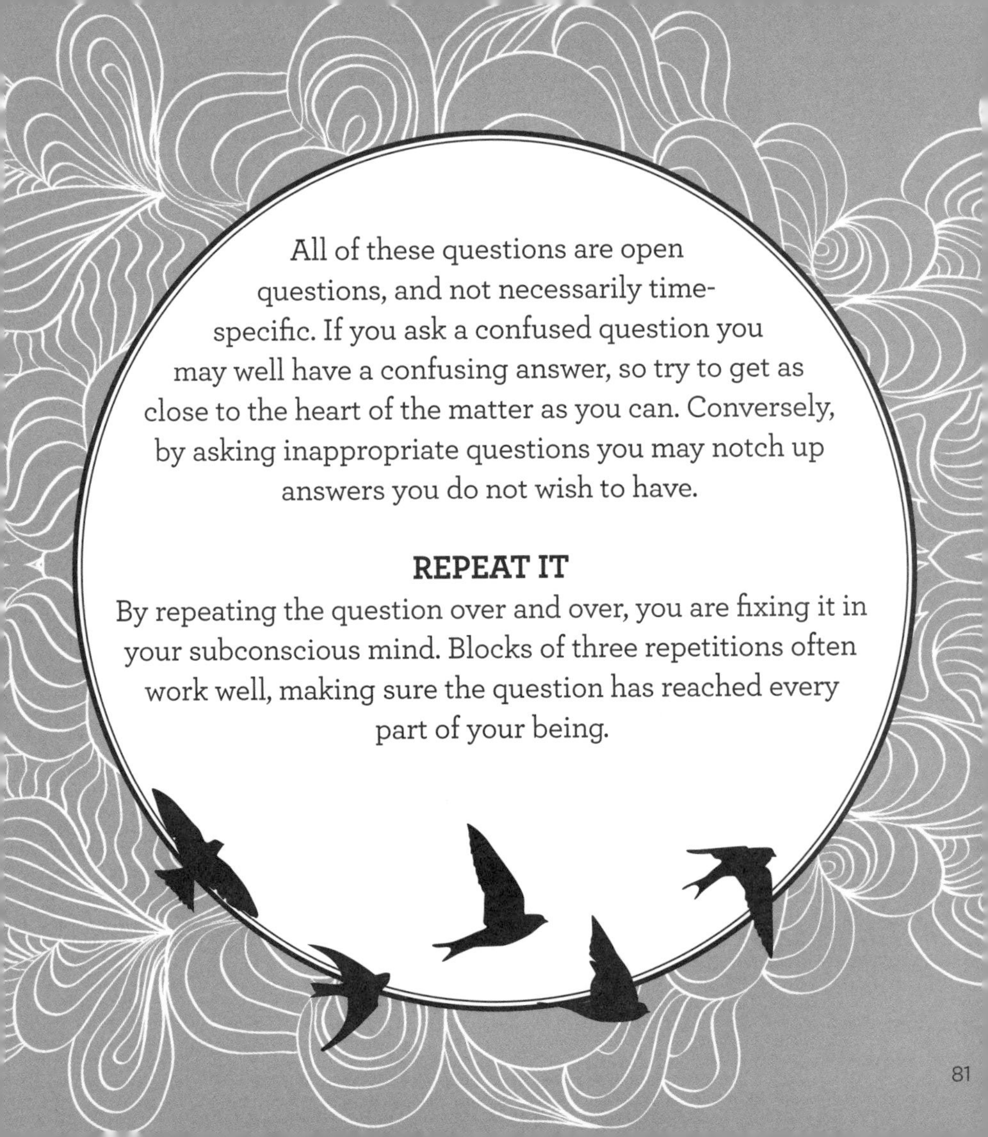

All of these questions are open questions, and not necessarily time-specific. If you ask a confused question you may well have a confusing answer, so try to get as close to the heart of the matter as you can. Conversely, by asking inappropriate questions you may notch up answers you do not wish to have.

REPEAT IT

By repeating the question over and over, you are fixing it in your subconscious mind. Blocks of three repetitions often work well, making sure the question has reached every part of your being.

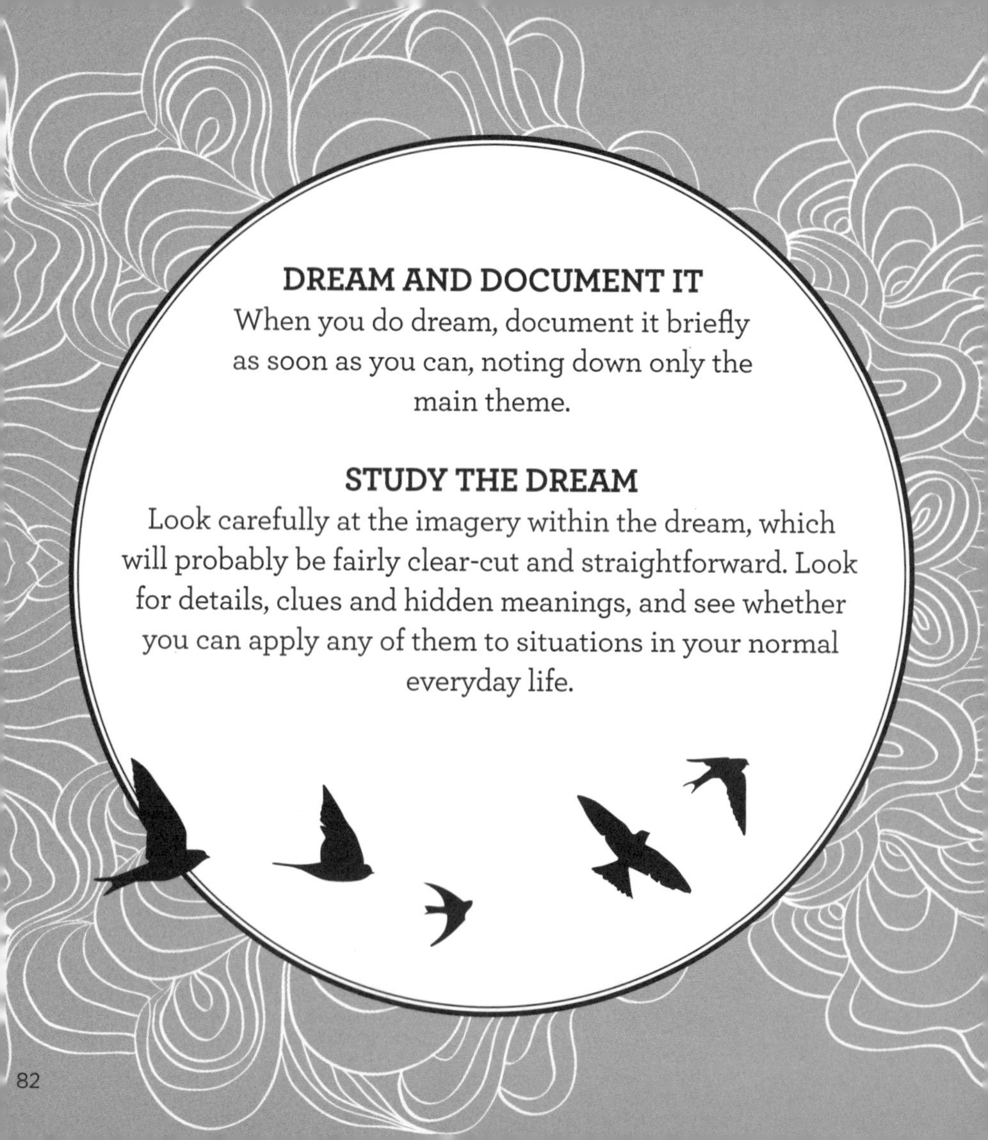

DREAM AND DOCUMENT IT

When you do dream, document it briefly as soon as you can, noting down only the main theme.

STUDY THE DREAM

Look carefully at the imagery within the dream, which will probably be fairly clear-cut and straightforward. Look for details, clues and hidden meanings, and see whether you can apply any of them to situations in your normal everyday life.

A word of
warning: the dreaming self is
quite capricious, so to begin with you
may not receive an answer on the night you
request it. You may only receive part
of an answer, or nothing for several nights,
and then a series of dreams which tell you
what you need to know.
This is a highly individual process, and no one can tell
you how it should be. With time you will recognize your
own pattern, but be prepared to be patient
with yourself.

HOW TO HAVE A LUCID DREAM

This technique is extremely simple and is used as a preparatory exercise to the MILD technique shown on pages 90–3. Lucid dreaming is a potent tool in dealing with our internal 'gremlins'. More importantly, it is a way of raising our consciousness and of developing our internal imaging in a very creative way. However, it is a technique which, unless you have hit upon it by chance, needs some training. Try not to be disappointed in the results you achieve at first; you will improve with practice if you have the patience.

• As you prepare yourself for sleep, give yourself the instruction that tonight you will have a lucid dream. Form an affirmation of intent along the lines of a very simple statement such as, 'Tonight my dream will be lucid'. Keep the statement as simple as this, because you are initially simply learning to 'go lucid'. The content of the dream does not matter at this point.

- Repeat your affirmation of intent either out loud or to yourself as many times as you need to in order to fix it in your own mind. This in itself is helpful, since it is teaching you how to focus your mind on one thing at a time. An affirmation is a simple, positive statement encapsulating as succinctly as possible what you intend to happen.

- Hold your intent in mind, and then allow yourself to drift off into sleep.

- When you wake up, note the time and whether you remember having been lucid. Also note how long you think you were in a state of lucidity. Your estimation will probably not be very accurate to begin with, but this does not matter, since you will become more proficient as time goes on.

REALITY CHECK

As your periods of lucidity become longer, you will find that there is a need to check whether you are truly dreaming or not. Probably the best way of doing this is to look at the ground, or at your own hands and feet, to see if they are as they should be.

- Ask yourself a question. The most sensible question to ask is, of course, 'Am I dreaming?' The simple asking of the question may initially be sufficient to chase away the dream, and you may well wake up. In time, you will be able to apply other techniques to allow you to stay within the dream
- Look at your hands and feet. Checking these for size and normality helps to stabilize the dream. If they seem larger or smaller than normal, then you are probably dreaming. In your dream, try to move them and watch what happens.
- Carry out an action that you know is impossible in real life. This could be anything from jumping into the air for

a huge distance to rolling up a hill. The important thing is that it needs to be an action which goes against the normal parameters of everyday life. If you perform the action, you are dreaming.

- Look at the ground or the dream scenario. If there are bizarre elements in either of these, you are probably dreaming. If you do not believe that what you are perceiving is real, then you are probably dreaming. You might ask yourself the question, 'Is this real?'

- Remind yourself that you are or have been dreaming. If you can, remind yourself during the dream that 'This is a dream'. Also, when you wake up, tell yourself, 'That was a dream'. Gradually you will come to recognize very quickly what is a dream and what is not.

A reality check is good to do even when you know you are awake. It helps to remind you that we live in a state of illusion anyway – that life itself is an illusion.

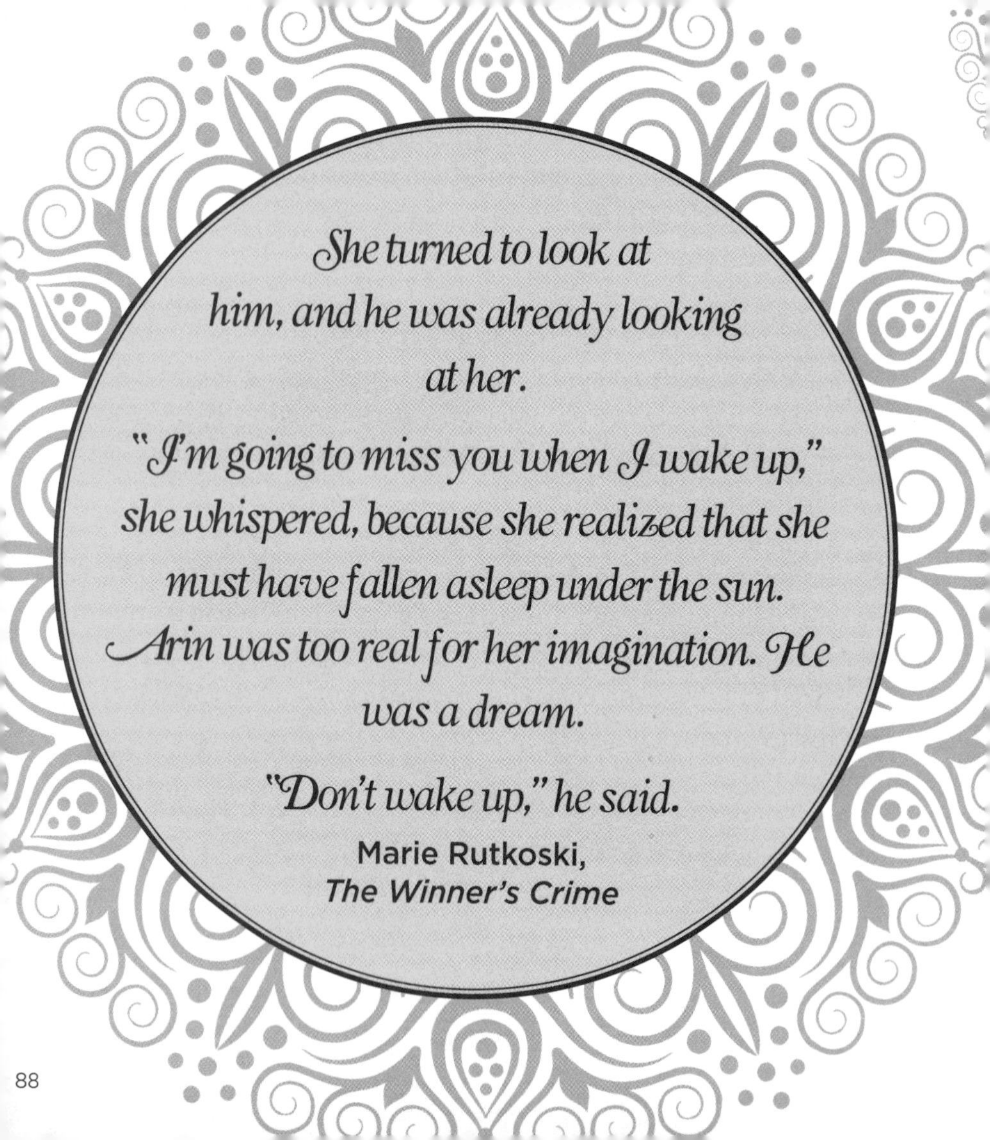

She turned to look at him, and he was already looking at her.

"I'm going to miss you when I wake up," she whispered, because she realized that she must have fallen asleep under the sun. Arin was too real for her imagination. He was a dream.

"Don't wake up," he said.

Marie Rutkoski,
The Winner's Crime

I had a dream about you last night. I was alone on a dark night and you came to me as a firefly. I knew it was you because you were the brightest.

Crystal Hudson, *Dreaming is For Lovers*

Dreams are stories made by and for the dreamer, and each dreamer has his own folds to open and knots to untie.

Siri Hustvedt, *The Shaking Woman, or A History of My Nerves*

THE MILD TECHNIQUE

The Mnemonic Induction of Lucid Dreams (MILD) technique was developed by psychophysiologist Stephen LaBerge and his colleagues during their investigations into creative dreaming in the 1980s. Most people who are interested in any type of dreamwork will have developed their own version of the technique, since the recall of dreams is a tremendous aid to personal growth. The steps are as follows:

1. Set up dream recall. Learn to wake up from dreams and to recall them. Initially, you may need to use an alarm clock, soft music or diffused light. Eventually you will be able to wake up at will by giving yourself the instruction to do so. When you do wake from a dream, try to recall it as fully as possible and, if necessary, write

it down or record yourself describing the dream.

2. Focus your intent. As you go back to sleep, concentrate intensely on the fact that you intend to remember to recognize that you are dreaming. Use an expression to fix this idea in your mind such as: 'Next time I'm dreaming, I intend to remember I'm dreaming.' Keep focused on this idea alone and don't allow yourself to be distracted by stray thoughts.

3. See yourself become creative. Perceive through your imagination that you are back in a dream you have had, whether it is the last one or another one that you clearly remember. Tell yourself you recognize it as a dream. Look for something odd or out of place that demonstrates plainly that it is a dream. Tell yourself 'I'm dreaming' and, knowing what it feels like to be dreaming, continue to remember your chosen

dream. Then imagine what your next lucid dream will feel like. See yourself carrying out your chosen plan. For example, note when you would 'realize' you are dreaming. See yourself carrying out a dream action such as flying or spinning around.

Repeat steps 2 and 3 until your intention is fixed, then drift off to sleep. Sometimes while falling asleep, your mind may wander. If so, repeat the steps so that the last thing in your mind before falling asleep is the thought that you will remember to appreciate the next time you are dreaming.

The MILD technique is designed to allow a dreamer to induce creative dreams at will at any stage during a night's sleep. Many people find that waking early and then dozing for another hour or so induces the best types of lucid dreaming, while others find that deliberately taking a nap at other times of the day has the maximum effect. The condition of the brain and body at the time of day when naps are to be taken needs to be just right to bring about lucidity – relaxed and aware. Probably the best time for creative dreaming is during the final period of sleep. In a full night's sleep, it seems that lucid dreams tend to be grouped towards the end of the night – or rather the early morning – and become more likely with each REM period of the night.

Experiments and dream diaries show that creative dreams are not evenly distributed throughout the night. It seems that a period of wakefulness just before an attempt to become lucid might help to focus the dreamer's attention on the matter in hand. Thus, the *intention* to dream lucidly also plays a part in the process.

PROLONGING A LUCID DREAM

One of the problems which occurs as we learn to have creative dreams is that we tend to wake up within a very short interval of realizing that we have become lucid. This problem does disappear the more adept we become, but it takes time and patience to overcome the initial hurdle. Most people develop their own methods of holding on to the awareness of lucidity, but there are also some tried-and-tested techniques that will work.

Each of the methods below have been found to be useful in prolonging the lucid dreaming state once you are ready to move on. Before trying them, you might wish to practise the relaxation and meditation techniques shown earlier.

- **SPINNING**
  As your original dream begins to fade, but before you become properly awake, try spinning on the spot. You should do this as rapidly as possible, beginning from an upright position. You should find that you either re-enter your own dream or spin to a new scenario.

- **CONTINUING AN ACTIVITY**
  When you find yourself in the middle of a lucid dream and it is beginning to fade, carry on with what you were doing in the dream but ignore the fact that the dream is losing clarity. As you continue with your activity, repeat over and over again to yourself, 'The next scene will be a dream.'

- **RUB YOUR (DREAM) HANDS TOGETHER**
  When you become aware that you are dreaming lucidly and the dream begins to fade, try rubbing your hands together very hard – you should experience the movement and friction. Continue rubbing your hands together until you wake up or the dream scenario shifts. Keep repeating a phrase which ensures you stay with the dream, such as 'I am continuing to dream.'

- **FLYING**
  This has much in common with spinning. You are inhibited only by your imagination. Experiment with flying in your own way, according to whatever you find most comfortable.

- **SENSORY MANIPULATION**
  Use your senses to help you to stay with the dream. Concentrate on each sense in turn and expand your awareness of each one. Listen, for instance, to your own breathing, and then become aware of other inner sounds and voices. Try holding a conversation with one of your dream characters.

It is quite important that you develop your own way of prolonging your dreams. You will find that you are more comfortable with one particular way, but you could try experimenting with the others just to see what happens.

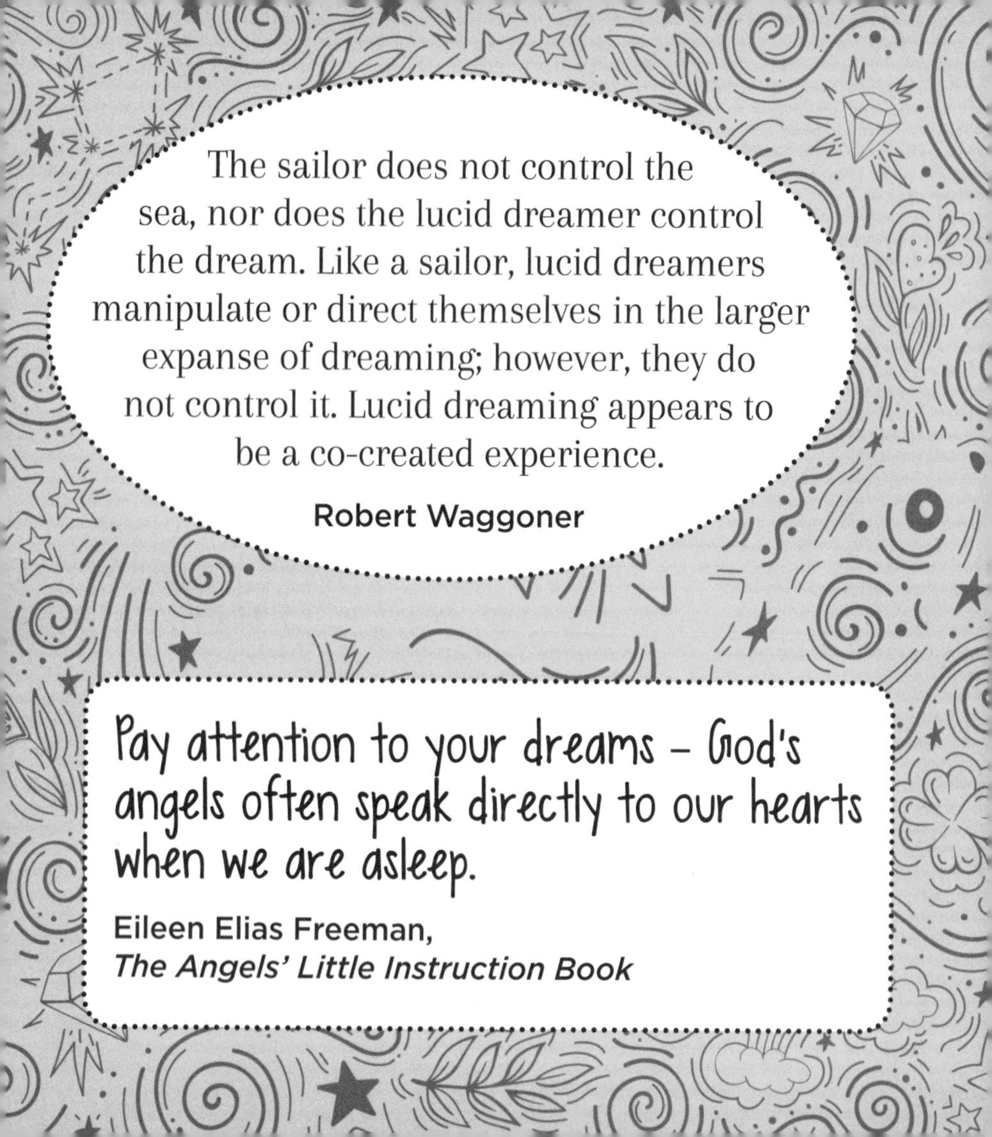

The sailor does not control the sea, nor does the lucid dreamer control the dream. Like a sailor, lucid dreamers manipulate or direct themselves in the larger expanse of dreaming; however, they do not control it. Lucid dreaming appears to be a co-created experience.

Robert Waggoner

Pay attention to your dreams – God's angels often speak directly to our hearts when we are asleep.

Eileen Elias Freeman,
The Angels' Little Instruction Book

Dreams say what they mean, but they don't say it in daytime language.

Gail Godwin

I think we dream so we don't have to be apart so long. If we're in each other's dreams, we can play together all night.

Bill Watterson

ANALYZING DREAM STRUCTURE

Whether your dream is lucid or otherwise, you will always need to analyze its structure. The more proficient you become, the more your dreams will begin to make sense and, as time goes by, you will begin to see certain themes and ideas repeated over and over. By keeping a dream journal, you will find that certain parts of a dream may well relate to segments of another dream, and an answer is hidden therein.

Begin by writing out the dream in your own words, splitting it into its component parts. In doing this, you need to decide how your dream may be divided into segments. Try to look for natural breaks that separate it into distinct parts, each with their own story. Take as an example the dream opposite.

'I was in a big building with a group of people and didn't know anyone. Somebody had been murdered by a member of the group I was with. We decided the murderer was the boy who was sitting in the corner on his own. We had to kill him because he'd killed someone in the group. We decided that he had to be stoned to death and we all joined in. A large cat appeared that ate everyone one at a time, as slowly as possible. But the cat had taken a liking to me, so he didn't kill me. Then I found out that the cat was really my best friend.'

This dream may be divided into the following parts:

- Where the dreamer was and how they felt.
- The action of the dream and the dreamer's inclusion in the group.
- What was happening to the group.
- The dreamer's realizations.

The next step in analyzing the dream structure is to decide which is the most important part. In this example, the most significant segment is the killing of the boy and the violence involved. We might give this part a title, such as 'Murder' or 'The Killing'.

After that, name all the other segments of the dream. The first part might be called 'The Building' or 'Setting the Scene'. For each title, it is important that the name resonates with you; allocating a title helps to fix the dream structure in your mind and improves your ability to recall your reactions in the dream.

It is also necessary to discover within each section whether you, the dreamer, are active (taking action) or passive (inert). In our example, the dreamer is passive and conscious of their lack of friends.

Looking closely at the dream in this way begins to uncover the similarities and differences between each segment. Much of this dream has an element of aloneness in it. At first, the dreamer knows nobody; the boy who kills is alone; and finally, the dreamer is again set apart. There is also violence and death in the main parts of the dream. Someone has been murdered and as a subplot the murderer must himself be violently killed by virtue of a group decision. At this point, however, the cat becomes an agent of death in that he (an individual) begins to eat (absorb) members of the group. The dreamer, also an individual, is saved by the fact that they realize that the cat is actually their best friend. Thus, one theme of the dream is uncovered – that of needing to belong, contrasting with the need to be an individual.

The differences in the segments are also recognizable. In the first section, the dreamer is alone and knows no one. In the second, they are a member of a group, and in the third, they are watching a lone cat absorb the rest of the group. In the last segment, it is the dreamer's relationship with the cat which is important.

Thus, another theme which is revealed is that of a meaningful relationship.

A further similarity/difference comparison reveals that while each section is indeed to do with death, the methods by which death comes are different. In the section to do with murder, a particularly primitive method is chosen by the group: that of stoning. In the segment to do with the cat, the method is 'natural' (a cat eats its prey) yet also bizarre. The cat eats the members of the group in a slow way, one after the other. This would tend to suggest that the dreamer has to be conscious of her need to face some kind of ending – which may possibly be violent – in order to achieve a different standing with someone who has the potential to be destructive. The general theme therefore seems to be the need for change in the dreamer.

Once the dream has been worked on in this way, the various themes can be listed and further work done on the symbols in each section which pick up these themes. In the first section of our example, our dreamer is aware of not knowing anyone. They also do not seem to know the boy accused of murder, nor initially do they know either the cat or the fact that he seems to be their best friend. Some useful consideration might be given through dreamwork as to whether the dreamer is something of a loner and how they react to the world in which they live.

There is an element of the absurd or bizarre in this dream, in that the dreamer unexpectedly recognizes that the cat is their best friend. It is at this point that the dreamer might have become lucid.

I had a dream about you last night… you were holding a pine cone and introducing him as Gerald.

Nicole McKay, *I Had a Dream About You*

Dreaming permits each and every one of us to be quietly and safely insane every night.

William Dement

Yet it is in our idleness, in our dreams, that the submerged truth sometimes comes to the top.

Virginia Woolf

For in dreams we enter a world that is entirely our own. Let them swim in the deepest ocean, or glide over the highest cloud.

J.K. Rowling, *Harry Potter and the Prisoner of Azkaban*

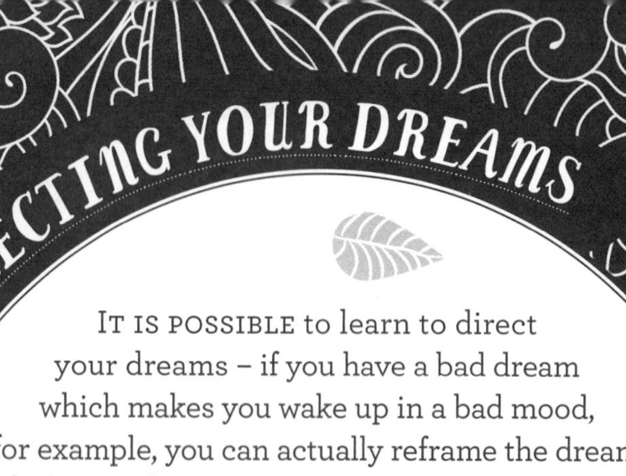

DIRECTING YOUR DREAMS

IT IS POSSIBLE to learn to direct your dreams – if you have a bad dream which makes you wake up in a bad mood, for example, you can actually reframe the dream and 'change the script'. Improving the outcome of a bad dream makes everything seem better and leads to better moods. Indeed, questioning and assessing your own state of consciousness is an established way of handling nightmares and night terrors.

A method known as the 'RISC technique' is an excellent way to direct your dreams. Developed in the United States in the 20th century as a therapeutic tool for dealing with bad dreams, the acronym stands for recognize, identify, stop the dream, and change the dream.

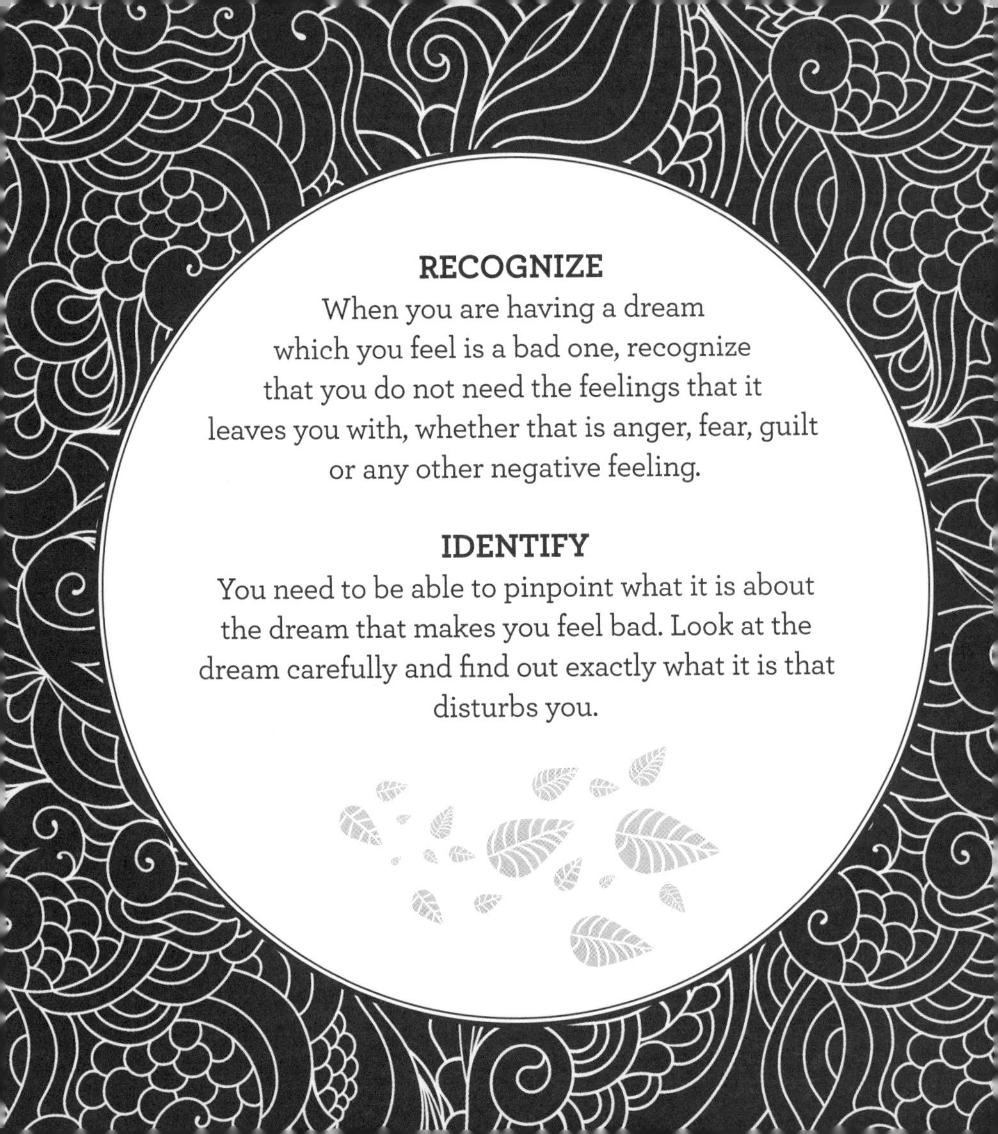

RECOGNIZE

When you are having a dream which you feel is a bad one, recognize that you do not need the feelings that it leaves you with, whether that is anger, fear, guilt or any other negative feeling.

IDENTIFY

You need to be able to pinpoint what it is about the dream that makes you feel bad. Look at the dream carefully and find out exactly what it is that disturbs you.

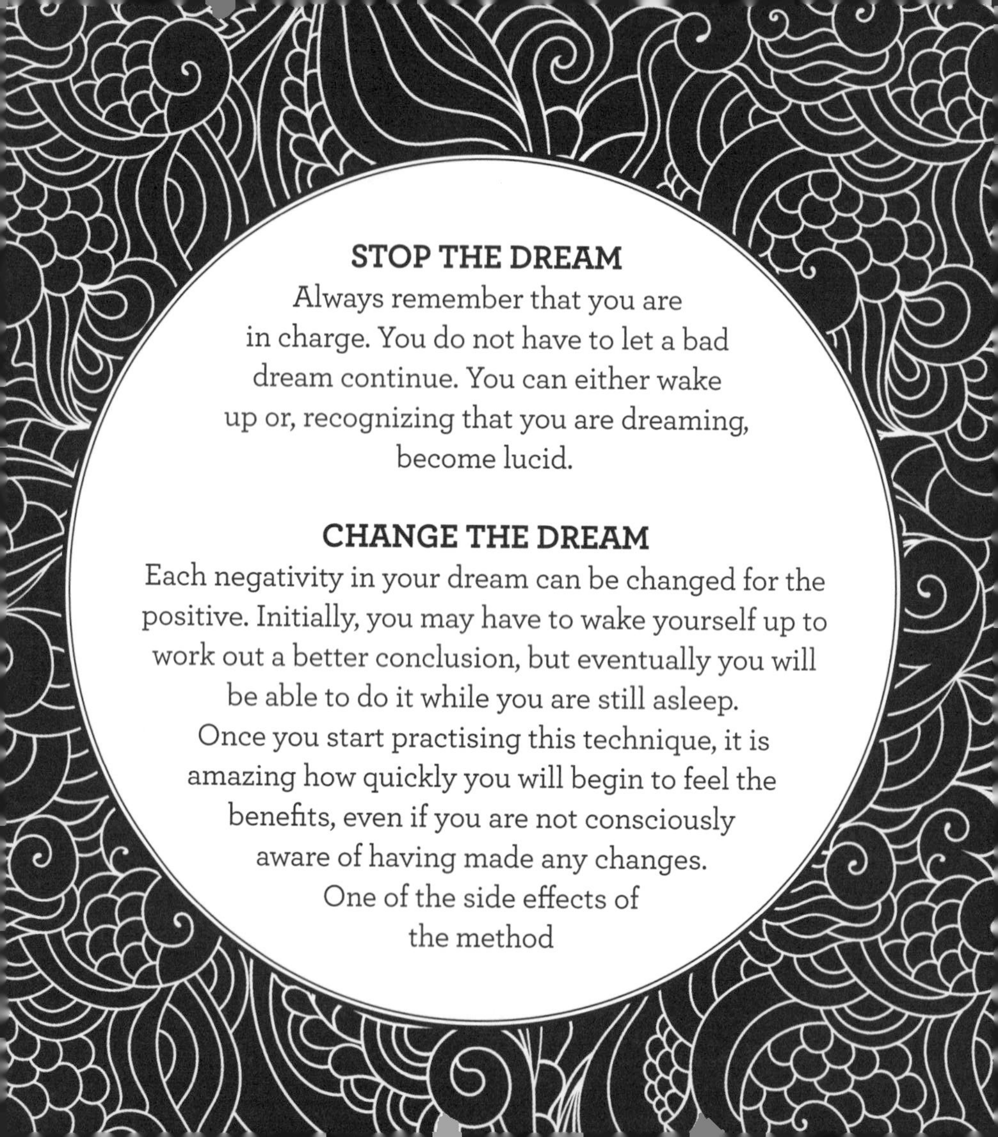

STOP THE DREAM

Always remember that you are in charge. You do not have to let a bad dream continue. You can either wake up or, recognizing that you are dreaming, become lucid.

CHANGE THE DREAM

Each negativity in your dream can be changed for the positive. Initially, you may have to wake yourself up to work out a better conclusion, but eventually you will be able to do it while you are still asleep. Once you start practising this technique, it is amazing how quickly you will begin to feel the benefits, even if you are not consciously aware of having made any changes. One of the side effects of the method

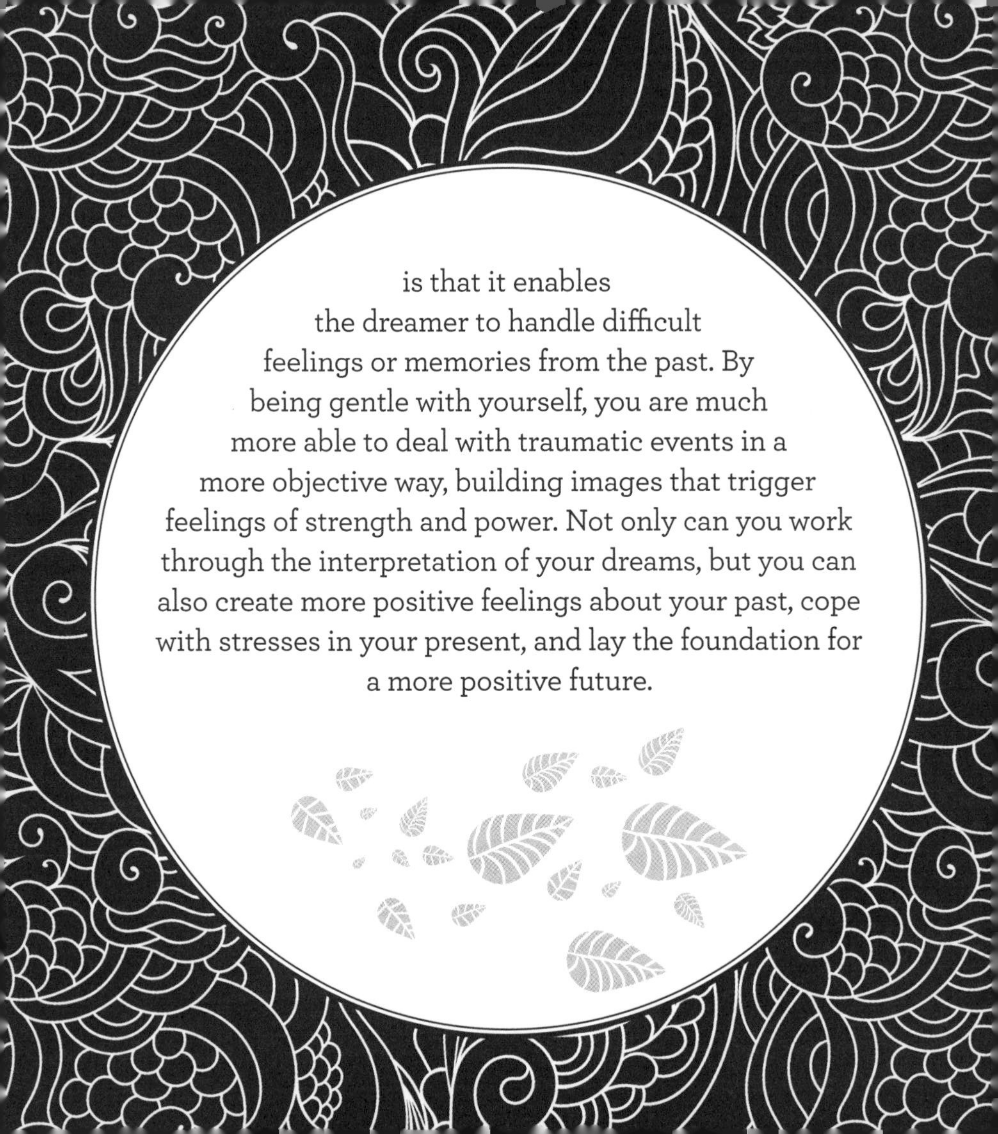

is that it enables
the dreamer to handle difficult
feelings or memories from the past. By
being gentle with yourself, you are much
more able to deal with traumatic events in a
more objective way, building images that trigger
feelings of strength and power. Not only can you work
through the interpretation of your dreams, but you can
also create more positive feelings about your past, cope
with stresses in your present, and lay the foundation for
a more positive future.

HEALING THROUGH DREAMS

Healing and dreams are very closely interlinked. Through dreams we are able to put ourselves in touch with the hidden, more unconscious parts of our personalities. We are capable then of healing a problem from within, rather than only dealing with the symptoms and their effects. For instance, something may have happened during our childhood which, because it is too difficult to handle, we have buried deep within us. Only when a similar trauma happens in adult life does that part of us who knows and remembers everything look through its records and present the original trauma in our dreams (often in symbolic form) for our consideration and attention.

When we have learnt to understand this process, and also the symbolism of our dreams, we can carry out

what is popularly called 'dreamwork' and heal that frightened, damaged part of ourselves. It is this damaged part that may be stopping us from having successful relationships, gaining a promotion at work or experiencing personal contentment. Dreamwork consists of being able to:

- Change your attitudes – either to yourself or your external world.
- Develop insight into what makes you the person you are.
- Solve problems and make choices in the light of such insights.

  Use your dreams constructively to change the reality of your everyday life.
- Deliberately choose to dream about something that is worrying you.

Many people believe they have healed themselves through the use of dreams, both lucid and otherwise.

Dreaming may enhance the body's own natural ability to heal, thereby creating an inner environment conducive to fast recovery. Dreaming may also help an individual come to terms with disability of one sort or another. The techniques of flying or spinning, both of which are used in lucid dreaming, are particularly helpful to people with physical disabilities, enabling them to experiment with the mental adjustments necessary for coping with the frustrations of mobility problems. On a psychological level, facing our fears through dreams can obliterate them altogether – it is as though the mind recognizes that it no longer has the power to distress the dreamer.

Not only can dreams be used for healing yourself, but with practice can be used to help other people too. Insight into somebody else's condition – physical or mental – can often come to you through dreams, because there is a part in all of us which is alive to subtle imbalances in the people and environment around us. Our own experiences may have given us clues and techniques to deal with such imbalances, and we can thus help the other person.

Some people are better able to interpret others' dreams through the use of intuition and knowledge of symbolism. In what might be called 'dream therapy', working in a group can help to heal. In this, meaningful dreams are shared with others for interpretation. It is then up to the dreamers themselves to choose the most relevant suggestions out of the many possibilities given.

Perhaps one of the most important ways of using dreams for healing is the recognition that individuals will almost inevitably try to make themselves better. Symbols of healing occur in dreams most often during times of illness, before or after surgery, or after a life crisis such as a family bereavement – at these times, the body and mind are doing their best to re-establish an internal balance. An example of such a symbol might be the image of leaking pipes at the onset of a heart condition.

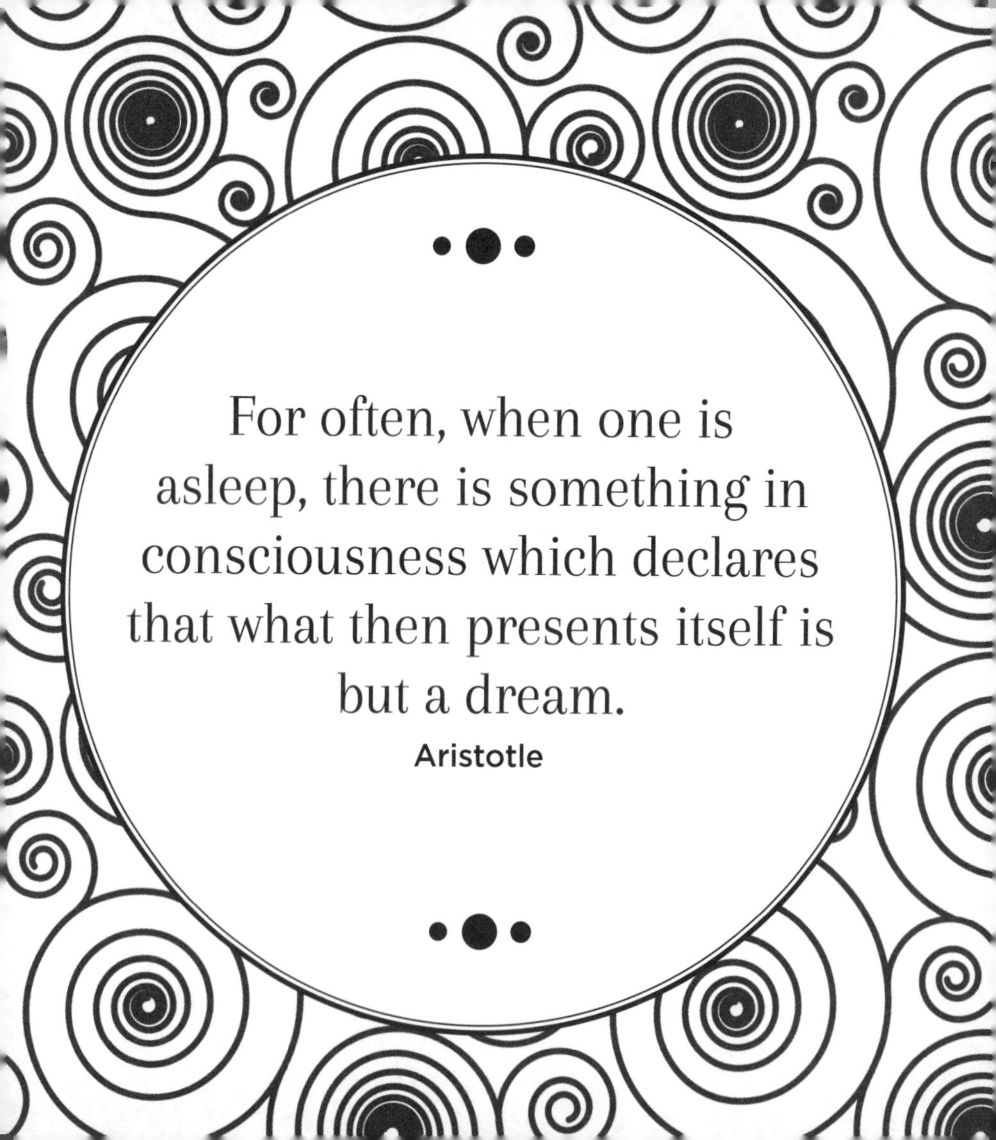
For often, when one is
asleep, there is something in
consciousness which declares
that what then presents itself is
but a dream.
Aristotle

I'll take the dream I had last night,
And put it in my freezer,
So someday long and far away,
When I'm an old grey geezer,
I'll take it out and thaw it out,
This lovely dream I've frozen,
And boil it up and sit me down
And dip my old cold toes in.

Shel Silverstein

COMMON THEMES IN DREAMS

PLACES AND ENVIRONMENTS

Much of the imagery to do with places and environments in dreams is easily interpreted simply by thinking about what that environment means to us. It may suggest a particular mood or feeling we experience in our day-to-day lives in those circumstances; being out in the open air, for example, will feel quite different from being in a factory or busy office, or in our own kitchen. Highly atmospheric, the environment of our dream can provide a framework for the images by establishing the mood of the dream and therefore of our state of mind.

The *countryside*, for instance, can suggest a feeling of freedom. To be in a *farmyard* in a dream shows us as being in touch with the down-to-earth side of ourselves. An *urban environment* or *industrial landscape* may well suggest stress and hard work or bustle and hurry. A *city* or *town* will signify an industrious frame of mind. When we dream of being in a *nightclub,* we are highlighting the right of every human being to belong.

Often the setting will echo our everyday concerns, perhaps being similar to our *place of work* or a place that is *easily recognizable*, such as a cemetery. The former might suggest that we need to take note of what is happening in our everyday environment. The latter would not always be to do with an actual physical death, but perhaps the final stages of a particular period in our lives.

When we become conscious of our environment being a particular room, such as a lounge, bedroom or kitchen, the personal relevance will be worth interpreting. A *lounge*, for instance, might be a place where we welcome others, a *bedroom* a place of relaxation, and a *kitchen* a place of nurturing.

THE SIGNIFICANCE

Often the setting or environment in a dream can give an insight into our state of mind. For example, a *landscape* that becomes *fertile or lighter* in the course of the dream suggests that circumstances around us may be changing for the better.

Dreary, unfriendly landscapes, or *tranquil, beautiful places* may well refer to our own subjective view of the world at that particular time. A *particularly dark and depressing atmosphere* can demonstrate the feelings that we have about a situation without necessarily being able consciously to express them.

Places that are familiar to us will evoke certain moods and memories. For instance, in dreams, *a childhood home or where we were born* suggests a secure space. However, if it now feels oppressive and it does not seem to be a sanctuary, we may no longer need such safety and reassurance.

A place that seems familiar and yet at the same time appears unknown suggests that there is a situation in waking life that is following an old pattern of behaviour. However, it has unknown elements within it which may help us to develop a different way of reaching a solution. *Unknown or unfamiliar places* usually represent aspects of a situation in waking life that have not yet made themselves apparent.

Characteristics within us that are too frightening or powerful to be allowed full expression in waking life are often perceived in dreams as *enclosed spaces*. *A space sheltered from the elements* offers a degree of peace and tranquility and may be an initial representation of the still, calm centre within. This calmness can also be represented by dreams of *outer space*, as we widen our perceptions.

BUILDING AND STRUCTURES

By their very nature, buildings and structures that appear in dreams call for different interpretations.

A *workplace or office* situation is slightly more formal than our home, and highlights our feelings about work and authority. A *library* is an important symbol suggesting the collective unconscious available to all humanity and the wisdom and skills that we have accumulated. A *museum,* however, denotes old-fashioned thoughts, concepts and ideas. It can also represent a place where we store our memories.

A *house* most often refers to the soul and our sense

of inner sanctuary, from which we can build our lives. Any *religious building* will similarly suggest a place of sanctuary and refuge, where we may be at peace with our beliefs and raise our own vibration to a more spiritual level.

A *hospital*, depending on our attitude to such places, may be a place of safety or perhaps one where we feel threatened and vulnerable. It is a healing, perhaps transitional environment or space, where matters physical, emotional or spiritual can be brought into a state of balance. *A hotel, guesthouse or bed and breakfast* place will also represent a transitional space, a place of temporary respite where we can be nurtured and cared for.

An image of a *tower* of any sort in a dream represents the personality and the soul within. While there are obvious connotations that connect it to masculinity and assertiveness, it is perhaps more accurate to perceive it as the self within the world in which we live. Since the building of a tower, particularly the *steeple of a church*, was initially designed to 'point to the heavens', the symbolism also indicates greater understanding of the spiritual self.

Any defended private space such as a *castle, citadel or fortress* may variously represent the feminine nature, a place of safety or our innermost intuitive self. It will sometimes suggest a fairytale or myth-like element in our perceptions. *Prison* or imprisonment of any sort

in dreams stands for the traps we create for ourselves, usually through a sense of duty or guilt.

The *pyramid* is one of the oldest constructions known to humanity, and is a very powerful image. In the physical realm it is a building that creates awe; mentally it symbolizes regeneration. The true point of power is considered to be in the centre of the pyramid, indicating our own inner potential. Thus, from a spiritual perspective, the pyramid is a guardian of power.

When a building in dreams is in *ruins*, we have to ascertain if it is through our own neglect or foolhardiness. If, however, the cause appears to be others' vandalism, we may be making ourselves vulnerable.

THE SIGNIFICANCE

Buildings in dreams generally are symbolic of the structures we build around us to help us manage our everyday lives. The attitudes and beliefs we have formed over the years from our own experiences and perceptions can appear as buildings or parts of buildings; a childhood house might, for instance, suggest a return to innocence or trigger memories that are relevant.

The beliefs and perceptions of others around us, such as our families and close associates, also play a part in those inner constructs that appear in our dreams. The surrounding environment in dreams will often also give us information that reflects our character, hopes and

concerns. Just as in waking life when we learn a lot about a person from their personal surroundings, we can also learn a great deal about ourselves through our dream constructions. Home, after all, is more relaxed than a work environment, the former highlighting personal concerns, the latter our more public persona.

Sometimes in dreams buildings can become composite – containing more than one element to be considered. To understand the relevance of composite images, we should interpret the main appearance of the building first, then the subsequent images as characteristics to be recognized and incorporated into our interpretation.

Dreams are more real than reality itself, they're closer to the self.

Gao Xingjian

I have always been amazed at the way an ordinary observer lends so much more credence and attaches so much more importance to waking events than to those occurring in dreams.... Man... is above all the plaything of his memory.

André Breton, *Manifesto of Surrealism*

I am accustomed to sleep and in my dreams to imagine the same things that lunatics imagine when awake.

René Descartes, *Meditations on First Philosophy*

A well spent day brings happy sleep.

Leonardo da Vinci

OBSTRUCTIONS AND OBSTACLES

Coming up against any kind of obstruction or obstacle is an extremely common and often revealing theme in dreams, referring to an obstacle of some kind in our lives.

A *hole in front of us* represents a difficult or tricky situation. A *pit, abyss or void,* however, is an aspect of the unknown which all of us must face at some time or another in our lives. Experiencing such an image in a dream demonstrates a fear of losing control, of a loss of identity, or of some type of failure. This fear of failure is a very strong emotion and can often also be represented in dreams by a *precipice or cliff.* This psychologically puts us on edge, or on the edge, requiring acknowledgement of the risks involved.

Barriers perceived in dreams are often self-imposed, more often being thought of initially in terms of 'I can't' rather than 'How do I get around this?' To be *standing on a border between two countries* shows the need to be making great changes in life, whether temporarily or otherwise, perhaps following different customs and culture. Interestingly, *turning a corner* in a dream can suggest that we have succeeded in moving forward into new experiences, despite what may have seemed to be obstacles in front of us.

Many dreams will depict the idea of *climbing a hill or mountain or of reaching a plateau*. The former suggests that we have reached a goal, or a point at which things must inevitably change, and perhaps become easier. In the case of the latter, we have not yet reached the end but can continue on our way without further challenge.

In dreams there are numerous objects or situations that represent obstacles. The object itself can often be relevant, as also can be the particular action or situation that occurs in the dream. A *cell or cage* normally represents some form of entrapment or imprisonment, perhaps of our

wilder instincts. We may also be aware of being trapped by the limitations of the physical body, or of being restricted by past experience. Often when we feel trapped in dreams, we are unable to break free of old patterns of thought and behaviour, although these may often be inherited patterns.

A *dam* might represent a sense of frustration or the bottling up of our own emotions whereas a gate can suggest a way through a problem. *The type of fastening* on a closed door or gate will often give us information as to how a difficulty can be overcome. If we are *opening a lock or padlock,* we may be trying to open up to new experiences. Both *gates and doors* signify a threshold experience, being at the commencement of a situation that requires a degree of courage to begin.

THE SIGNIFICANCE

Through dreams we are often able to recognize that there is a problem or an obstacle to progress in waking life. Any obstruction in a dream alerts us to the fact that we cannot, at this stage, reach our goal or achieve a successful outcome. We perhaps have to consider why this is, or even whether the goal itself is appropriate. We must decide whether the obstruction or obstacle has simply arisen of its own accord, whether it has been deliberately placed there either by us or other people, or whether it is an integral part of the dream scenario. This will help us to uncover the root of the problem in everyday life.

There are times when our own inhibitions and anxieties can only be faced when we give them tangible forms. Difficulty, indecision and doubt are three main blocks that occur in life; dreams may give us information as to how we need to tackle the problem. Obstacles in dreams can therefore take on many forms – *a wall, a hill, a dark forest, a pit* and so on. If the obstacle appears insurmountable, then we must consciously find our way around it; if it is too difficult to get over, then we may need to use other ways of dealing with what it represents.

POSITION

We can learn much from where things are in relation to us as dreamers, so it is valuable to consider this when looking at the position of characters, articles or environments.

When we dream of anything *higher or above us,* our spirit, intellect, ideals and consciences are being brought to our attention. Anything *underneath, below or downstairs* signifies the more mundane concerns, and perhaps the most basic issues we have. Being aware of *something behind us* will often highlight the past, as well as suggesting support in the here and now. *Something in front* usually indicates being drawn forward or belonging to our future. Anything *to the right* represents the more dominant logical aspect of our waking self. It is the consciously expressed, confident, more objective side. When we are drawn *to the left,* it suggests the less dominant, more passive intuitive aspect of our nature. When we cannot decide between *left and right,* it suggests an inability to choose whether to rely on drive or instinct.

THE SIGNIFICANCE

When a particular position is highlighted in a dream, it usually signifies our moral standpoint or our position in life. It can also give an indication of how we are handling situations in our lives. For instance, *something in the wrong position* means we are going about things in the wrong way. If we are aware of anything *appearing upside down*, it emphasizes the potential for chaos and difficulty. The 'ups and downs' of situations in life can be experienced in dreams as the actual movement of our position. Having our attention drawn to *a backward movement* usually indicates the potential to adopt a regressive backward-looking tendency. *Looking or moving forward* suggests that we focus on the future. Dreaming of *something that is far away* may indicate that it is far away in time. This may be future or past, depending on other elements of the dream. *A long way in front* would be future; *a long way behind* would be past. *Near or close* would mean recently, or in the immediate present.

Dreams are true while they last, and do we not live in dreams?

Alfred Lord Tennyson

The interpretation of dreams is the royal road to a knowledge of the unconscious activities of the mind.

Sigmund Freud

NATURE, ECOLOGY AND PLANTS

Vegetation in a dream can often represent the underlying abundance and fertility that is available to us and our capacity for growth. *Cultivated ground*, such as a *garden*, can indicate an area of life where we are nurturing our potential, whereas a patch of *weeds* would suggest a neglected area of our personality. Mental attitudes and old patterns of behaviour that clog us up and do not allow us to move forward can very often be shown in dreams as weeds. For instance, a patch of *brambles* can suggest irritating snags to our movement forwards, whereas *nettles* might represent people actually trying to prevent progress.

If the *plants are simply growing wild*, there is a part of us that needs freedom. If they are grown in *regimented or formal rows*, we are overly concerned about other people's views and opinions. In dreams, *seeds* represent great potential and latent power. *Grass or turf*, particularly if it is uncut, suggests fresh opportunity. As a marker of time, the traditional *sheaf of corn*, a symbol of consolidation and of binding, will suggest autumn – a time of harvest.

Trees in dreams can have particular meaning. A tree with *wide branches* would suggest a warm, loving personality, whereas a *small, close-leafed tree* would suggest an uptight one. A *well-shaped tree* would suggest a well-ordered person, while a *large, messy tree* would suggest a chaotic being. A *forest* traditionally is frequently a place of testing and initiation, an unknown space and threshold

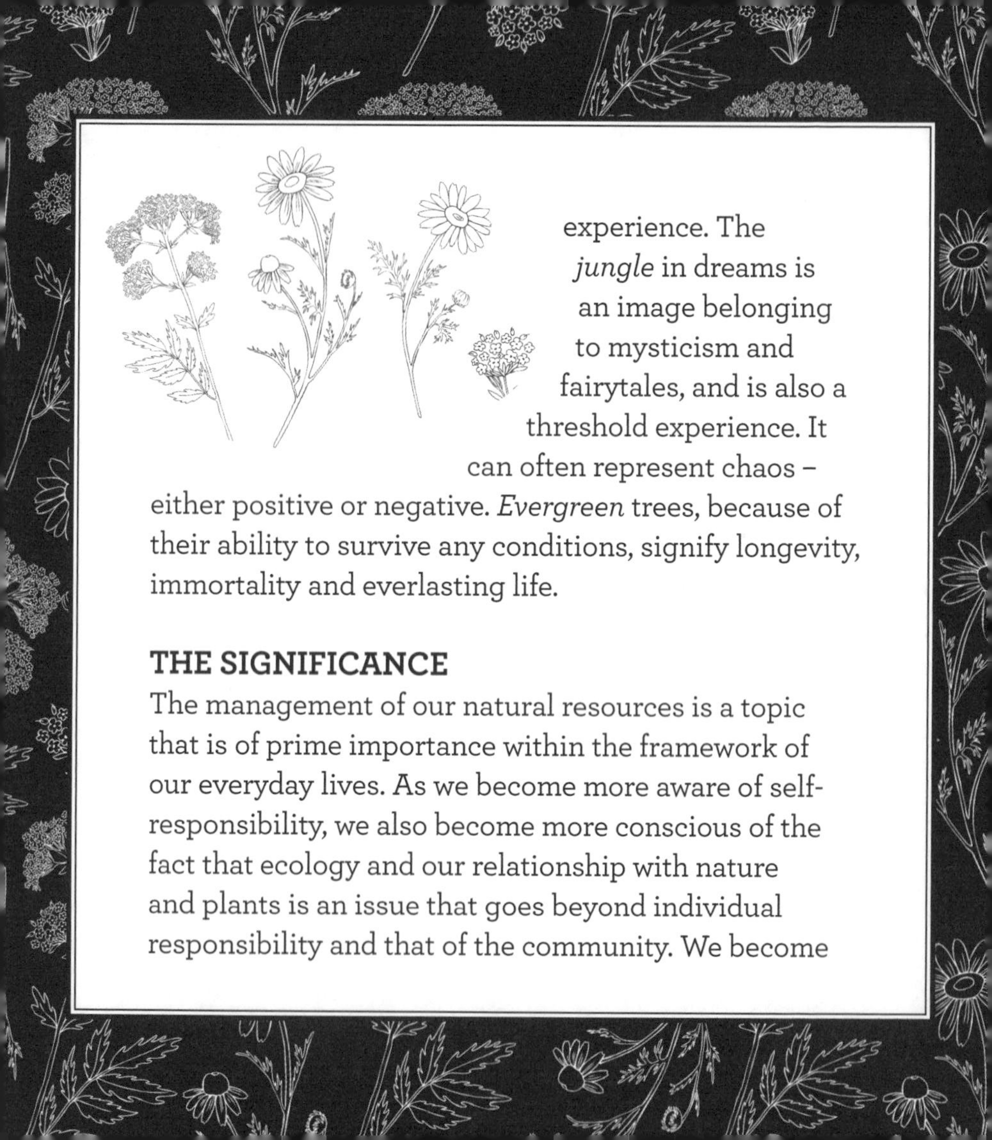

experience. The *jungle* in dreams is an image belonging to mysticism and fairytales, and is also a threshold experience. It can often represent chaos – either positive or negative. *Evergreen* trees, because of their ability to survive any conditions, signify longevity, immortality and everlasting life.

THE SIGNIFICANCE

The management of our natural resources is a topic that is of prime importance within the framework of our everyday lives. As we become more aware of self-responsibility, we also become more conscious of the fact that ecology and our relationship with nature and plants is an issue that goes beyond individual responsibility and that of the community. We become more passionate about the survival of the world as we know it, and show a deeply felt response to the misuse of resources.

Often our dreams will demonstrate such concern, and the representations of nature become more significant. *Plants*, for instance, signify the life force and cycle of life. Because of their process of growth and decay, they become a symbol for progressive change. Flowers of any sort can indicate love and compassion. *Bouquets, bunches of flowers, garlands and wreaths* all signify honour to one degree or another. Garlands and wreaths in particular, because they are circular, suggest continuity and sometimes commitment.

As more people become aware of ecological issues and children in particular internalize the need for the responsible use of resources, dreams about *ecology* demonstrate a passion for the world in which we live.

A dream which is not interpreted is like a letter which is not read.

The Talmud

Those who have compared our life to a dream were right ... We sleeping wake, and waking sleep.

Michel de Montaigne

Dreams are excursions into the limbo of things, a semi-deliverance from the human prison.

Henri Amiel

It is a common experience that a problem difficult at night is resolved in the morning after the committee of sleep has worked on it.

John Steinbeck

NUMBERS, SHAPES AND PATTERNS

Each of us has an instinctive appreciation of the esoteric meaning of numbers, shapes and patterns and, with a little study, can enhance the interpretation of our dreams by using that knowledge.

Numbers naturally led to the science of measurement, and there is within that field a branch of measurement called sacred geometry, or the 'measurement of perfection'. Religious buildings of all sorts – *churches*, *temples* or *mosques* – show some aspect of this measurement of proportion, that is, the relationship of the part to the whole.

Over time, certain shapes and patterns have acquired a symbolic meaning. The *dot* symbolizes the central point, from which everything starts. The *circle* is a two-dimensional representation of unity and perfection, the inner-being or the self. In many ways the *sphere* is the simplest and most perfect of forms, a three-dimensional solid. Usually appearing as a globe or ball, in dreams it suggests perfection and completion of all possibilities. The *oval* is formed by the intersection between two interlinking circles. It symbolizes where the spiritual and physical worlds meet – a very powerful energized space. Associated with the moon, the *crescent* represents the feminine, mysterious power that is intuitive and non-rational. It may be shown as either waxing (becoming larger) or waning (growing smaller). The *spiral* is symbolically the perfect path to evolution. The principle is that everything is continually in motion, but also continually rising up or raising its vibration.

The *triangle* can be a representation of the family – mother, father and child – but probably more often symbolizes body, mind and spirit. The *square* signifies the manifestation of spirit into matter. It represents the earthly realm as opposed to the heavens. As a solid object, the *cube* signifies mundane concerns, stability and physical manifestation.

The *cross* is one of the most common structures in Western cultures. The stem of the cross, the vertical line, stands for the heavenly or spiritual, while the transverse beam represents the material physical plane. A *diamond* shape appearing in a dream indicates that we have options available, some of greater value and some lesser. The *star*, particularly if it is a bright one, indicates an individual's hopes, aspirations and ideals. It is those things we must reach for.

THE SIGNIFICANCE

Almost all ancient systems recognized the significance and power of numbers, both as single digits and, when combined in particular ways, even more powerful figures. They could also be used to signify something else – a kind of code that could hide information from those who were not privy to it and reveal it to those who were.

Leonardo Pisano, who lived at the turn of the 13th century, is better known by his nickname Fibonacci. The *Fibonacci numbers* and also *fractals* (complex geometric patterns) have huge significance in the understanding of numbers and numbering, because the ability to count, and the patterns in nature, are largely based on these two principles. Fractals are present in inorganic structures such as clouds and coastlines and in living structures – even in unexpected places such as the circulation or intestinal systems in mammals. At some point or another, numbers and fractals will almost certainly appear in dreams.

Often in dreams what appears to be totally chaotic actually has an inherent sense of order, and it is this ordering that is perhaps most important. The patterns that appear as part of the scenario in dreams can categorize how we handle repeated behaviours in our lives. In some patterns, the basic figure that is repeated over and over again draws our attention to the significance of numbers and the symbolism of shape. The patterns that are repeated in nature, such as the patterning on a snake's skin or the repeated regularity of ferns as they grow, are in their own way small miracles of creation.

As we come to have greater access to our own creativity, we learn to accept the nature of things as they are. We can look at the fundamental structure of our own natures; we can appreciate the basic shape our life is taking without placing emotional inhibitions in the way.

SIGNIFICANCE OF NUMBERS AND SHAPES

This table is a brief analysis of number and shape significance in dreams, showing some traditional meanings.

NUMBER	SHAPE	SIGNIFICANCE
0	Cipher	Nothing, the Absolute
1	Unity	Oneself, the first
2	Cross	Balance, opposites
3	Triangle	Freedom, triad
4	Square	Stability, practicality, manifestation
5	Pentagram	Change, action
6	Hexagon	Harmony, balance, efficiency
7	Heptagon	Magical forces, spirituality, consciousness
8	Octagon	Infinity, spiritual and physical unity
9	Nonagon	Descent of spirit into the mundane
10	Decagon	Completion, fresh energy

COLOUR

Colour in dreams can be highly significant. It can either be true to life, or so bizarre as to need interpretation by relating it to our circumstances and to the symbolism of colour.

An example of a bizarre instance of colour might be that a yellow banana would be totally normal, whereas a blue one would require quite some consideration. While apparently completely inexplicable, a little thought will reveal the meaning: blue is a healing colour, suggesting relaxation.

By tradition, *black* holds within it the potential for all colours. Rather than being negative, in dreams it suggests absorption and the ability to make use of all available resources. *Blue* is the colour of a clear sky and is also the primary healing colour. *Brown* is the colour of the earth and also represents grounding and stability. *Green* is the colour of nature and of plant life. It also suggests nourishment of the self, particularly of our aspirations and desires. There is probably no true *grey*, only shades of the mixture of black and white, which in dreams will suggest degrees of negativity and positivity. *Magenta* is a colour that links both the material and the spiritual realms. *Orange* is an essentially cheerful, uplifting colour. *Yellow* is the colour that is closest to sunlight, the life-giving force. As a golden colour, it suggests prosperity and best use of earthly resources. *Red* suggests vigour, strength, energy, life, sexuality and power. *Turquoise* is a clear greenish blue, which in some religions is the colour of the freed soul. In its iridescent form it will represent, for many, a kind of spiritual attainment. *Violet*, while found by some to be too strong and rather overwhelming, retains its connection with royalty and means noble actions, especially for the greater good. *White* contains all colours and when passed through a prism gives us the colours of the rainbow. In dreams, this can represent the stages of growth we go through as we reach maturity or progress on our journey.

THE SIGNIFICANCE

Colour plays a vital part in all symbolism. This is partly to do with ancient traditions and also the vibratory frequency that each individual colour posesses. Colour actually affirms the existence of light, and once the colour spectrum was discovered, the vibrational energy of the *colours of the rainbow* could be given meaning. Scientific experiments have been carried out to ascertain what effect colour has, and have proved what healers have always known: colour can have a profound effect on mood and wellbeing.

In working consciously with the *colours of the rainbow*, we discover that the warm, lively colours – which give back light – are yellow, orange and red. Cold, passive colours are blue, indigo and violet. Green is a synthesis of both warmth and cold. Black absorbs all colour, while white light holds all colour in it. From a spiritual perspective, this balance provides a backdrop to the whole of existence.

They should invent some way to tape-record your dreams. I've written songs in my dreams that were Beatles songs. Then I'd wake up and they'd be gone.

Alice Cooper

Some colours exist in dreams that are not present in the waking spectrum.

Terri Guillemets

A ruffled mind makes a restless pillow.

Charlotte Brontë

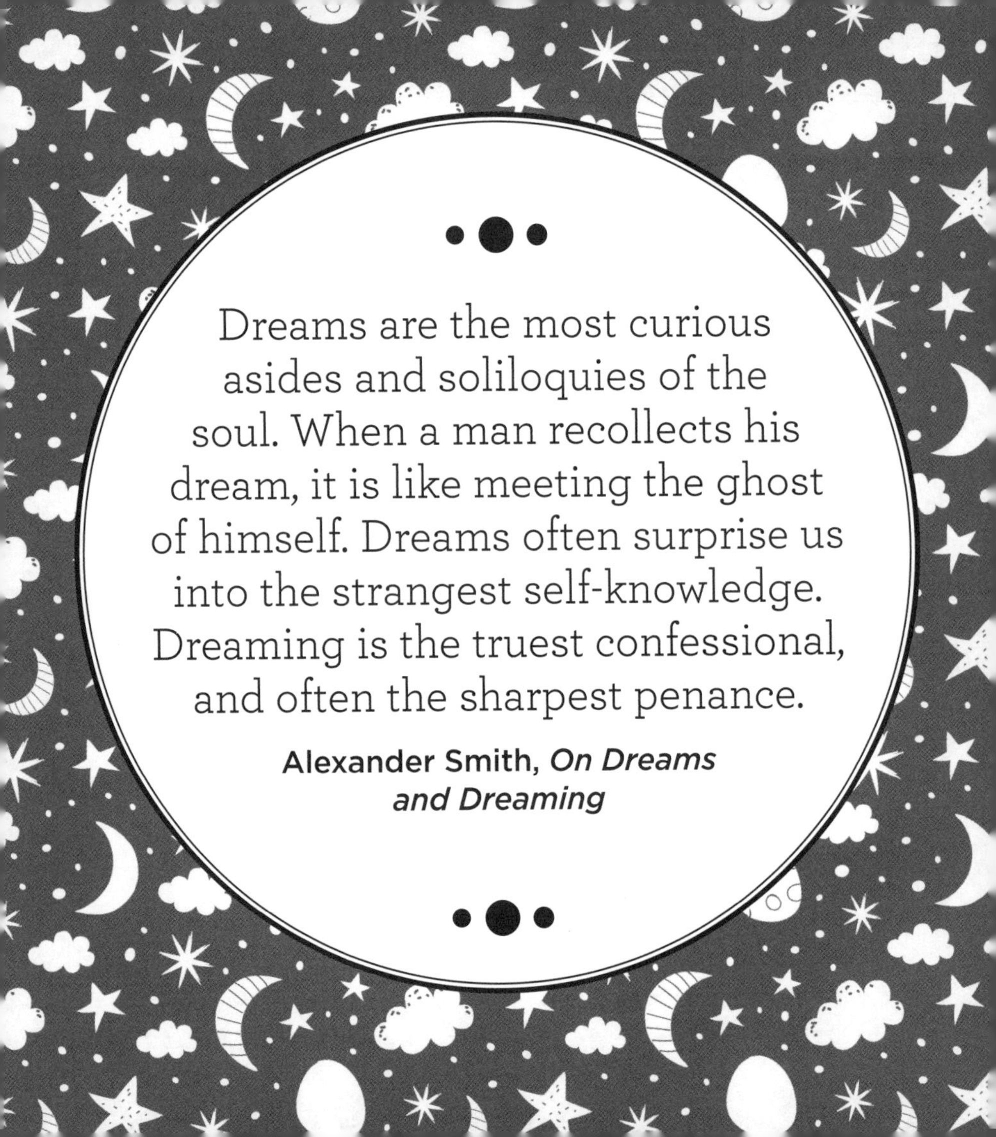

Dreams are the most curious asides and soliloquies of the soul. When a man recollects his dream, it is like meeting the ghost of himself. Dreams often surprise us into the strangest self-knowledge. Dreaming is the truest confessional, and often the sharpest penance.

Alexander Smith, *On Dreams and Dreaming*

TIME

With the mind freed from everyday constraints, time is usually immaterial: time in a dream may seem 'over in a flash', or action can seem to take place over a long period. In many ways, however, we are so tuned into diurnal and seasonal rhythms that these do achieve a symbolism in dreams.

To dream of a *dawn* or a *new day* represents a new beginning or a new awareness, usually bringing with it a sense of hope in circumstances around us. The *evening* can be a synonym for *twilight* and the boundaries of our conscious mind. It may also signify old age and wisdom.

Night signifies a period of rest and relaxation. It also symbolizes the darkness that occurs before rebirth or initiation, a fallow period where we gather energy for a new project. It can, however, also suggest a time of chaos and difficulty. Dreaming of *both day and night* indicates the cycle of time or of changes that will inevitably take place. When we become conscious of the seasons of the year in dreams, we are also linking with the various periods of our lives: *spring* signifies childhood; *summer* young adulthood; *autumn* our middle age; and *winter* represents old age.

Images connected with the measurement of time can have particular relevance in dreams. A *clock face* usually will alert us to the passage of time, a sense of duty or of urgency. An *alarm clock* literally sounds a warning of some sort, while a *digital clock or watch* alerts us to the significance of the numbers shown. An *electric timer*, such as that used to clock in to work, might indicate a measured period of hard work, while a *kitchen timer* would suggest nurturing or a creative period ahead. An *hourglass* – frequently seen in computer games – could indicate that time is running out in some way, or it could represent the passage of life, experience or old age.

THE SIGNIFICANCE

Strictly, because the mind is free from constraints in dreams, time is unimportant. If time is deemed to be significant in a dream, it is usually necessary to measure it in some way. Usually we are only aware of the *passage of time*, or that a particular length of time is meaningful in the dream – it is part of the dream scenario. Dreaming of *something that measures time* often alerts us to the need for us to measure our thoughts and activities.

When we consider dream content, the time may symbolize a particular time in one's life. The *daylight hours* will thus suggest our conscious waking life; where *several days* (or other long periods) seem to pass, some other activity in which we are not involved has been going on. The *hours of the day* could refer to a time in our life, or it may simply be the number of the hour that is important, so we should look at the significance of the numbers we notice (see pages 146–51).

SIGNIFICANCE OF TIMES OF DAY

Specific times of the day tend to have particular meanings.

TIME	SIGNIFICANCE
Morning	The first part of our life or our early experiences
Midday	Fully aware and being conscious of our activities (living mindfully)
Afternoon	Putting experience to good use
Twilight or dusk	A period of uncertainty and possible ambivalence; also a period of transition
Evening	Being more relaxed about life
Night	Being introspective or at rest; also a period of low energy or secrecy
Midnight	A change of pace or of focus

WEATHER

BECAUSE THE WEATHER is such an integral part of our everyday lives, it can go almost unnoticed in dreams, but it often highlights a particular theme or idea.

Storms, thunder and lightning all have an innate connection with the element of fire and are much to do with passion of one sort or another. This could be negative, in the sense of an outburst of aggression and rage, or positive in the sense of a blinding flash of inspiration or some kind of spiritual catharsis. The *sun*, while also connected with fire, is more connected with the giving of life. *Wind, hurricanes, tornadoes, gales and whirlwinds* are all connected with air. Air represents the intellect or driving spirit, so any of these weather features appearing in dreams suggests a deeply experienced revelation, sweeping all before it and causing a radical change in perspective.

Any *weather condition connected with water* will usually highlight our emotional state. In its simplest meaning, *rain* stands for tears and emotional release. *Hail,* because it is frozen rain, signifies the freezing of our emotions. *Snow,* however, is a crystallization of water, and as such represents the pleasing crystallization of an idea or project. When *melting,* it can represent the softening of the heart and emotions. *Ice* is a representation of rigidity. It is the brittleness that comes from not understanding what is going on around us, of creating circumstances where people cannot get in touch with us. Existing in isolation because of the way our lives have gone can also be symbolized by *icicles.*

A *glacier* or *iceberg* would suggest the inexorable forces of our nature.

An *earthquake* represents some kind of imminent upheaval, perhaps a loss of inner security. On a spiritual level, *an eclipse* can suggest a loss of faith in oneself, but also a sense of being ignored or not noticed. To dream of being in a *fog or mist* marks our confusion and inability to confront or even see the real issues in our lives. We are often confused by external matters and the impact they may have on us emotionally. A mist may also signify a state of limbo, a transition or a change in awareness.

THE SIGNIFICANCE

Weather, being part of the environment of the dream, usually indicates our moods and emotions. Different types of weather may be symbolic of a deeper inner response to external conditions. Through recognizing the weather conditions in dreams, we can become very much aware of changing external situations. We have to be careful to adjust our conduct in response to these. By being forewarned in such a way of external factors, we can develop the ability to control internal moods and emotions that may help us deal with these factors. Being aware of the seasons and the changing weather associated with them draws attention to new growth or opportunities, success in projects we have around us, harvesting of our efforts and conservation of energy. Being aware of the weather would also indicate the need to recognize that we are part of a greater whole.

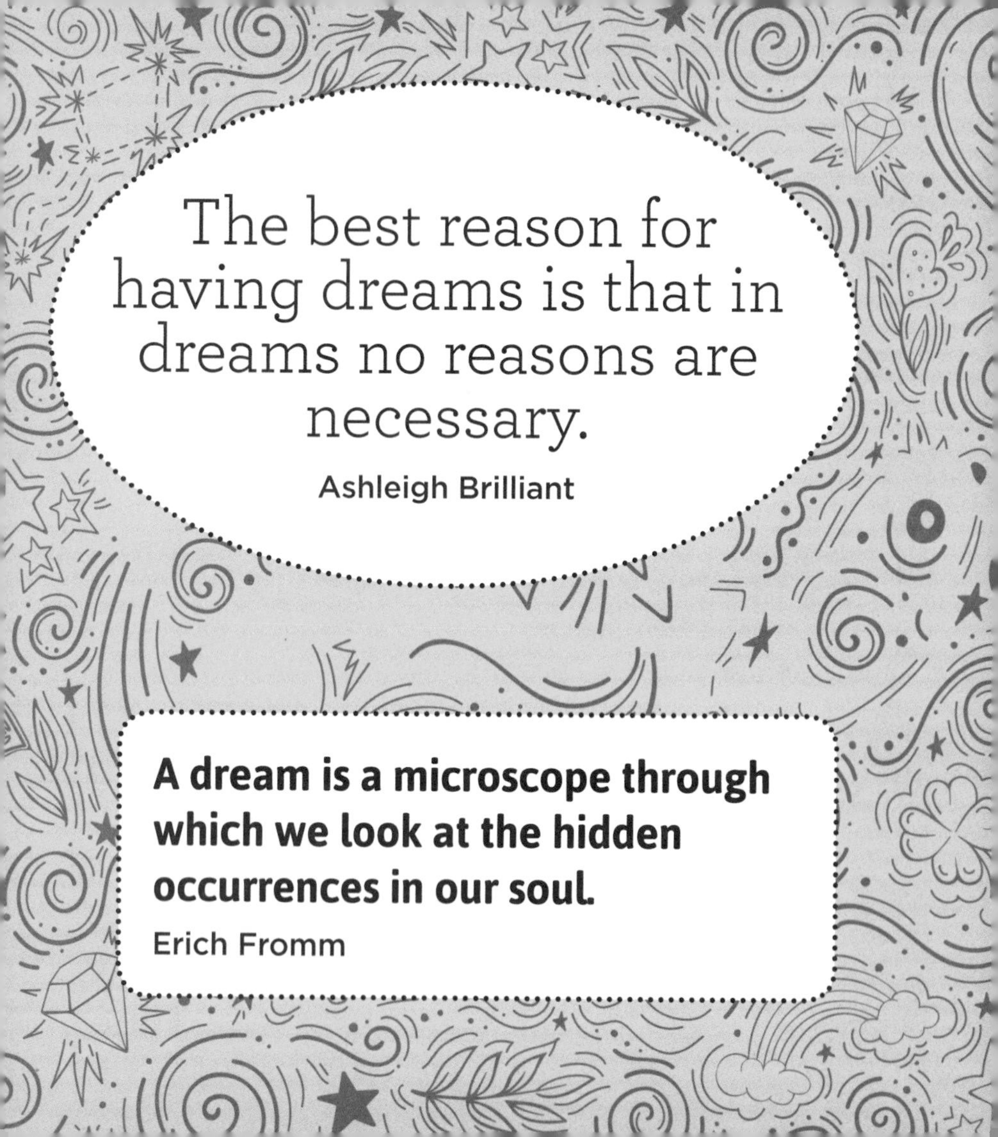

The best reason for having dreams is that in dreams no reasons are necessary.

Ashleigh Brilliant

A dream is a microscope through which we look at the hidden occurrences in our soul.

Erich Fromm

Sleep that knits up the ravelled sleave of care

The death of each day's life, sore labour's bath

Balm of hurt minds, great nature's second course,

Chief nourisher in life's feast.

William Shakespeare, *Macbeth*

WATER

THERE ARE SO many aspects to water that it is often necessary to perceive it differently according to its place in the dream. A *sea or ocean* usually depicts total knowledge – the not yet explored. It also represents the 'great unconscious' and our emotional connection to the 'ultimate', whatever we consider that to be. Being aware of *the tide* in the sea suggests that we need to be more aware of the ebb and flow of life in general and perhaps the passage of time. Indeed, any *current* will highlight the speed with which we live life and with it the potential for change. A *body of water* such as a *lake, lagoon, pond or pool* can signify a stage of transition between the conscious and the emotional self, or alternatively between the latter and the spiritual realms. Interestingly, the domain of the mysterious darker side of the feminine is often pictured as a lagoon in myth and

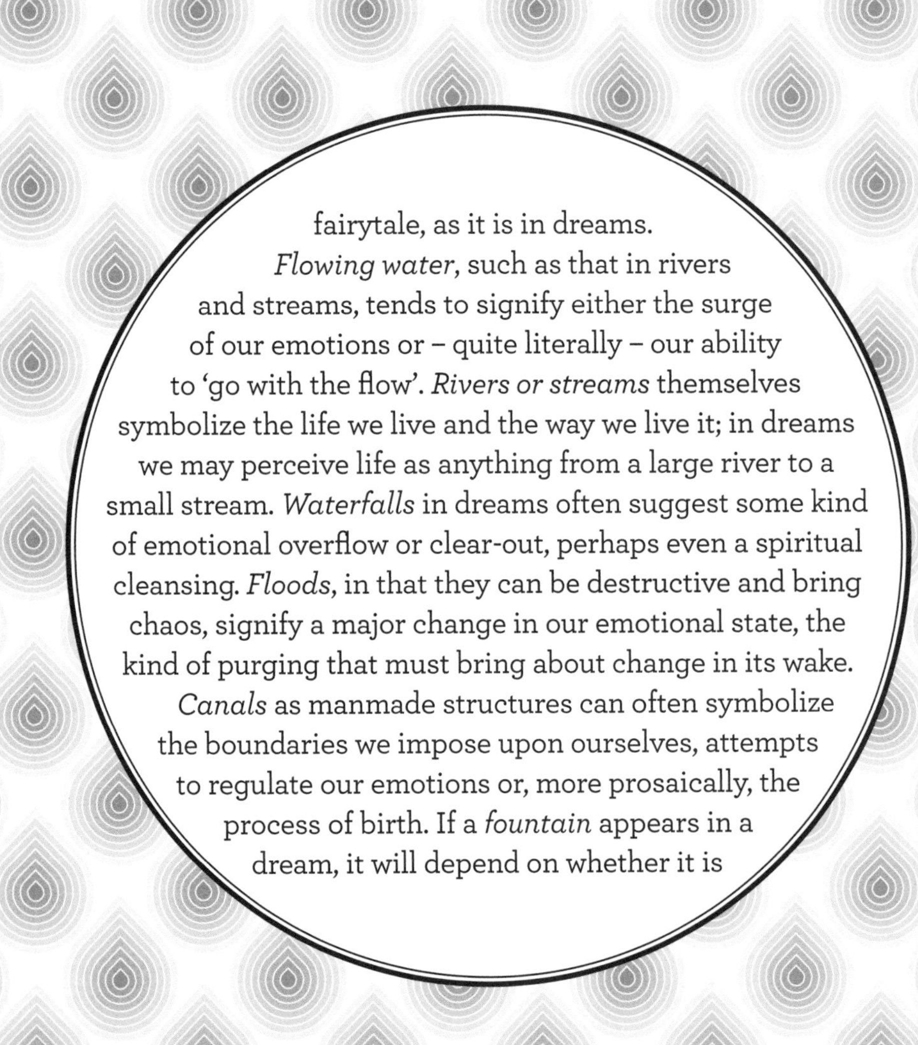

fairytale, as it is in dreams.

Flowing water, such as that in rivers and streams, tends to signify either the surge of our emotions or – quite literally – our ability to 'go with the flow'. *Rivers or streams* themselves symbolize the life we live and the way we live it; in dreams we may perceive life as anything from a large river to a small stream. *Waterfalls* in dreams often suggest some kind of emotional overflow or clear-out, perhaps even a spiritual cleansing. *Floods*, in that they can be destructive and bring chaos, signify a major change in our emotional state, the kind of purging that must bring about change in its wake.

Canals as manmade structures can often symbolize the boundaries we impose upon ourselves, attempts to regulate our emotions or, more prosaically, the process of birth. If a *fountain* appears in a dream, it will depend on whether it is something natural – like a geyser – or if it is manmade. If the former, it is often representative of a breakthrough in understanding our own emotions. If the latter, it is a channelling of our emotions in order to achieve more mastery over our circumstances. Fountains may also be taken as symbols of womanhood.

THE SIGNIFICANCE

Water is usually taken in dreams to symbolize all that is emotional, feminine and intuitive. In that it seeks its own level but also has movement in its flow, in dreams it can act as a gauge of our emotional state and the flow of emotions – conscious and unconscious. *Deep water* would thus represent a depth of emotion or perhaps the potential for us to be out of our depth in some way; *rushing water*

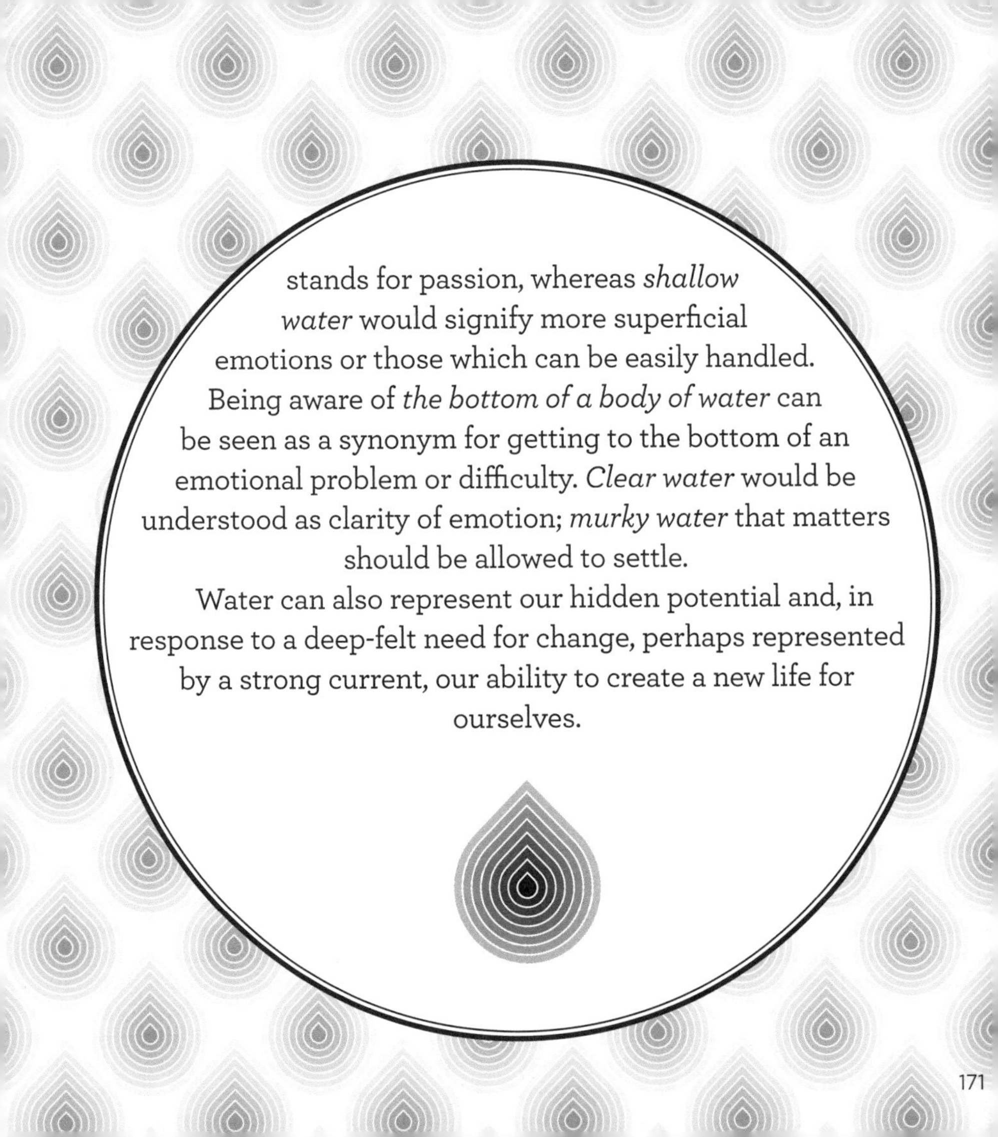

stands for passion, whereas *shallow water* would signify more superficial emotions or those which can be easily handled. Being aware of *the bottom of a body of water* can be seen as a synonym for getting to the bottom of an emotional problem or difficulty. *Clear water* would be understood as clarity of emotion; *murky water* that matters should be allowed to settle.

Water can also represent our hidden potential and, in response to a deep-felt need for change, perhaps represented by a strong current, our ability to create a new life for ourselves.

PEOPLE

When a person appears in a dream scenario, they are like an actor in a play, being there to convey an idea or a concept. It is thought that almost every character who appears in our dreams ultimately reflects a part of our own personality. Such characters can often be better understood if, during interpretation, we put ourselves in the position of that person. Rather than asking the character what they are doing in your dream, it can be illuminating to shift perspective and consider the dream from the character's point of view.

Dreaming of ourselves as an *adolescent* suggests that we concentrate on the undeveloped, perhaps immature, side of our personality. We might ask ourselves whether we need to support that part, give it expression in waking life, or allow it to mature by using the techniques of creative visualization and meditation.

Our impression of authority is usually first developed through our relationship with our father or father-figure. If we have had a domineering father, a *dictator or king* may appear in dreams as representing that relationship. Often, depending on how we were treated as children, our view of authority will be that it is anything from a benign helper to an exploitative disciplinarian. Most authority figures in dreams will ultimately lead us back to what is right for us, although not necessarily what we might consider good; our wilder, more renegade side needs controlling. To dream about a *baby*, particularly *one that we feel to be ours*, highlights those vulnerable feelings over which we have no control. We may also be considering a new project or way of life that is literally 'our baby'. If the *baby is someone else's* in the dream, we need to recognize that a situation in waking life is not our responsibility or that we should not interfere.

Dreaming of a *child* gives us access to the less developed sides of our personality – the inner child at a specific stage of development. We all have parts of ourselves that are still child-like and inquisitive. Dreaming of *our own children* highlights the special dynamic inherent in all family relationships and bonds.

A dream about a *boy* shows the potential for development through new experiences and being in touch with ourselves at a young age and with the unsophisticated naivety and passion that a boy has. We are connecting with our natural drives and ability to face difficulties. When a *girl* of any age appears in our dreams, we are usually attempting to make contact with the more sensitive, innocent, intuitive, feminine side of ourselves. If the girl is *known to us,* we probably are aware of those qualities but need to explore them more fully. If she is *unknown,* we can acknowledge that a fresh approach from a different perspective would be useful. In dreams, the

elderly very often represent either our forebears or ancestors, and hence wisdom accrued from experience. Our conformity, ways of behaving and ethics are largely handed down from generation to generation. *People older than us,* who are not necessarily elderly, usually signify our parents or some form of parental control. *Groups of elderly people* frequently appear in dreams and signify the traditions and wisdom of the past – those things which are sacred to the 'tribe' or family.

THE SIGNIFICANCE

A particular person's appearance in a dream may be significant because of the very ordinariness of the occasion, or alternatively because their behaviour is bizarre. This may be because the dreaming self wishes to highlight a particular aspect of either their character or actions in waking life. Dream characters may emphasize aspects of our occupation or indeed may even offer explanations of past actions. Only you as the dreamer will, with practice, be able to understand the significance to you.

Any *masculine figure* that appears in a dream demonstrates an aspect or facet of our essential being, usually our drives or the more logical side of our personality. *A man in a woman's dream* suggests that she is becoming aware that she has, or can develop, all the aspects of the masculine that enable her to reach her full potential. If the man is *one she knows or loves*, she may be trying to understand her relationship with him. An *unknown man or stranger* is generally that part of our personality that is not yet recognized. *A well-built or large man* appearing in our dreams indicates either our appreciation of the strengths, certainties and protection which our basic beliefs give us, or suggests that we may be feeling threatened or are made apprehensive by those very qualities.

Any *woman* appearing in a dream represents all the qualities that we understand as feminine. Such a figure in dreams can suggest the softer, more intuitive aspects of the personality. In *a man's dream,* such a figure describes his relationship with his own feelings and perhaps how he relates to his female partner. In *a woman's dream,* a female family member or friend in particular is often representative of an aspect of her own nature, but one she has not yet fully integrated. More spiritually, a *goddess or holy woman* signifies the highest aspect of the feminine that can be attained. It usually suggests intuitive wisdom and the need to work for the greater good. An *older woman* most often represents our mother and her sense of inherited awareness and wisdom, as epitomized by the crone or wise woman.

In a dream you are never eighty.

Anne Sexton

Dreams are real while they last — can we say more of life?

Havelock Ellis

We are such stuff
As dreams are made on,
and our little life
Is rounded with a sleep.

William Shakespeare, *The Tempest*

Believe in your dreams.
They were given to you for a reason.

Katrina Mayer

FAMILY

Images of our family and people we know appear frequently in dreams. Studies have shown that women tend to dream of family 15 per cent of the time, and men nine per cent.

Those considered to be close family are representative not just as themselves, but also of aspects of the dreamer's personality. The *father* or *father-figure* thus represents the masculine principle and that of authority, law and order, while the *mother* or *mother-figure* signifies the nurturing, protective principle. In a man's waking life, the father tends to become a role model for his behaviour and how he lives his life. In a woman's life, the father is the blueprint on whom she bases all later relationships with the masculine.

Other members of the *extended family* can also

represent specific concepts and ideas. For instance, *grandparents* appearing in dreams denote not only our attitude to them as people, but also to the traditions, beliefs and inherited characteristics handed down by them; they can often represent old-fashioned values. *Grandchildren* appearing may be an aspect of life affirmation, a passing on of traditions or a promise of better things to come.

THE SIGNIFICANCE

Images of the family, being the first people we relate to, have a great deal of significance in dreams. The family structure is the first secure image that a child latches onto. We know, for instance, that generally a man's first close relationship with a woman is with his mother or mother-figure; similarly, a woman's first relationship with the masculine is usually with her father or father-figure.

All our future relationships, both intimate and platonic, are influenced to some degree by the ones we first develop within the family. Thus, our position within the family will also influence our perceptions. Sometimes, through circumstances not within our control, such as illness, death or separation, those relationships can become distorted. Later dreams will either attempt to confirm the distortion or, as we reach a mature understanding, put this image right.

Almost all of the problems we come across in life are mirrored within the family, so in times of stress we will often dream of previous problems or scenarios that have been experienced, or our dream will remind us of that familial situation. When such dreams happen on a fairly regular basis, it is perhaps time to address the initial difficulty. It is as though a pattern is laid down which, until it is consciously challenged, will continue to appear. *Rivalry between siblings*, for instance – a common problem in life and in dreams – can usually be revealed as a feeling of insecurity and doubt, possibly relating to whether we feel we are loved enough within the family set-up.

The antagonistic patterns of behaviour between family members are fairly distinctive, and it is often easier to work these through in dreams rather than in waking life. Very early on in life, a child moves through extreme self-involvement and interest to an almost exclusive relationship – usually with the mother.

Next comes a different relationship with the father or father-figure, who clearly has an existing relationship with the mother, sometimes being perceived as a threat. Therefore, we may dream of *arguing with a family member*, but the significance depends both on other aspects of the dream and also our everyday relationship with that person.

SIGNIFICANCE OF FAMILY MEMBERS

Family members in a dream represent aspects of the dreamer's personality.

FAMILY MEMBER	SIGNIFICANCE
Father or father-figure	Largely an authority figure, whether benign or otherwise
Mother or mother-figure	Nurturing and caring, although may be destructive
Parents	Initial relationship template, possible role reversal as parents age
Husband	A woman's inner masculine traits, drive etc
Wife	A man's inner feminine traits, sensitivity etc

Brother	Similarity or rivalry
☾ Older ☾ Younger	Experience and authority Vulnerability or rivalry
Sister	Sensitivity and similarity
☾ Older ☾ Younger	Capability and caring Sibling rivalry or inappropriate behaviour
Son	The need for self-expression, parental responsibility
☾ In a father's dream ☾ In a mother's dream	Unfulfilled hopes, dreams and desires Her own ambitions, sense of continuity and perhaps disappointments
Daughter	Supportive relationship
☾ In a father's dream ☾ In a mother's dream	Fears of vulnerability Potential rivalry and/or friendship

ANIMALS

Animals appear frequently in dreams, and usually represent aspects of our personality that can be most easily understood on an instinctive level. By returning to instinctive behaviour, we are able to realign ourselves with our own inherent life force. This imagery and symbolism in dreams can be easily perceived once we realize that there is a degree of anthropomorphism involved; we invest our animals with very human qualities – the lion being considered regal, for instance.

Here we have included some familiar animals that tend to appear in dreams. These include domesticated and farmyard animals as well as some wild animals. By understanding animals and their symbolism, we are able to approach life in a simpler and more natural fashion. Some animal images have negative interpretations and others positive. Equally, what the animal is doing will influence whether or not there is a positive meaning to the image.

The *cat* often denotes the capricious side of the

feminine. The refined but also the powerful yet self-reliant aspect of woman may also be suggested. When a *dog* appears in dreams, we can recognize a devoted and loyal companion or a protector, but to dream of a *pack of wild dogs* portrays emotions and feelings of which we are afraid.

Fish generally signify both temporal (worldly) and spiritual power. Dreaming of fish connects not only with our emotional side but also our ability to be wise without being strategic, to go with the flow. To be dreaming of *fishing* suggests we are searching for information.

The figure of a *horse* in dreams represents our intrinsic vitality. Traditionally, a *white horse* describes our state of spiritual awareness, whereas a *brown* one represents our more rational and sensible side; a *black horse* is our excitable side. A *pale horse* suggests death, and a *winged horse* depicts the soul's ability to transcend the earthly plane. *Falling off* a horse suggests we have not yet controlled the energy inherent in our more powerful side.

The *lion* can represent the developing ego and the associated feelings and emotions. In its more negative connotation, the *leopard* represents oppression and aggression and, traditionally, the underhandedness of power wrongly used. If it is the spots that are noticeable, there may be a situation in our lives that cannot be changed. A *fox* can represent a degree of cunning needed in order to succeed.

A dream of a *mouse* shows there may be an aspect of chaos 'gnawing' at us in waking life. In the sense that they are unwanted and invade others' space, any *vermin* represent a negativity that needs to be got rid of. The *rat* in particular can represent something that is repellent or gnawing away at us in some way. A *white rabbit* may show us the way to the inner spiritual world and, as such, act as a guide.

The *ram* signifies the qualities of leadership necessary within a flock or group and therefore can represent the dedication needed for such a task. The *sheep* is renowned for its flock instinct, and it is this meaning – the need to belong to a group – that is most usually accepted in dreams. To dream of sheep and wolves, or of sheep and goats is to register the conflict between good and evil.

THE SIGNIFICANCE

Animals tend to surface in dreams as messengers from the unconscious. It is interesting to note that, from a cultural perspective, it is those animals with which we are most familiar that will tend to appear in dreams.

Looked at from a cognitive perspective, such dreams are ways of getting to know parts of ourselves that we have hitherto rejected or not understood. It was not until the 20th century, when psychoanalysts began to explore dreams more fully, that the connection with the cognitive mind was made. Nowadays it is easy to see why an animal image will alert us to some aspect of ourselves that we need to integrate more fully into our personality.

TOTEM ANIMALS

A totem is a natural object or animal that has personal symbolic meaning, and with whose energy we feel an affinity. Today, as we rediscover the simplicity of this connection, we too can create those links; such animals will make their appearance initially in dreams.

ANIMAL	TOTEM MEANING	SYMBOLISM
Bear	Power of the unconscious	All-caring mother
Bull	Fertility, relationship	Sexual passion, creative power
Cow	Nurturing	Eternal feminine, power of the group/family
Deer	Gentleness, innocence	Pride, nobility, status
Donkey/Ass	Wisdom, humility	Patience, obstinacy, determination

Elk	Strength, nobility	Stamina
Fish	Knowledge, determination	Worldly and spiritual power
Fox	Shapeshifting, invisibility	Crafty behaviour, cunning
Giraffe	Farsightedness	Expression, communication
Goat	Surefootedness, reaching fresh ground	Creative energy, masculine vigour
Hare	Leaps of faith	Intuition, spiritual insight
Hedgehog/ Porcupine	Defence against negativity	Tenacity, strength of purpose
Jackal/ Coyote	Wisdom, folly	Transformation of negative energy into positive
Jaguar	Courage	Balance of power
Kangaroo	Responsibility	Motherhood, protection, strength
Lamb	New life, sacrifice	Innocence

Lemming	Valour, use of available resources	Balance, introspection
Leopard	Invisibility	Stealth, hardiness
Lion	Leadership, honour	Dignity, strength, courage
Lynx	Inner secrets, hidden knowledge	Objectivity, clarity of vision
Monkey	Communication	Inquisitiveness, mischief
Moose	Awareness, sensitivity	Power, energy
Mouse	Attention to detail	Shyness, reticence
Otter	Playfulness, joy	Resilience, sensitivity
Ox/Buffalo	Right action	Hard work, untiring
Puma/ Cougar	Responsibility, empowerment	Grace, strength

Rabbit	Family, mothering	Fertility, sensuality
Ram	New beginnings	Energy, authority
Sheep	Purity	Group support
Squirrel	Preparation, activity	Hoarding, guardianship
Tiger	Passion, devotion	Dignity, power
Wolf	Guardianship, hierarchy	Teaching, free will

WILD VERSUS DOMESTICATED

Generally, totem animals are wild rather than domesticated so the significance of seeing a cat or a dog in your dream is unlikely to hold the same meanings as if you saw a leopard or a wolf. This is due to the relationships we have with animals in our everyday life and the symbolic meaning they hold for us in dreams.

Codi: So you think we all just have animal dreams. We can't think of anything to dream except our ordinary lives.

Loyd: Only if you have an ordinary life. If you want sweet dreams, you've got to live a sweet life.

Barbara Kingsolver, *Animal Dreams*

Dreams are free therapy, but you can only get appointments at night.

Terri Guillemets

Even thus last night, and two nights more I lay,
And could not win thee, Sleep, by any stealth:
So do not let me wear to-night away.
Without thee what is all the morning's wealth?
Come, blessed barrier between day and day,
Dear mother of fresh thoughts and joyous health!

William Wordsworth

BIRDS

By tradition, birds are powerful symbols and have a place in most cultures as having a strong connection with the divine. They have had significance to humans ever since we first began to observe their behavior – they were seen to symbolize certain qualities and powers, many of which have relevance even today.

White and black birds can represent any polarity in our waking lives so, symbolically, Noah's action in sending out a black bird and a white bird signified the end of one kind of belief system and the beginning of another. In other imagery in dreams, a *caged bird* can indicate some kind of restraint or entrapment; a *pet bird* can denote some dearly loved principle or ideal that we are unable give up; and a *flock* of birds represents a group purpose or ideal.

A bird's *plumage* is its protection, but it is also its power and strength. In a dream, plumage being drawn to our attention can often stand for a display of power and strength, and may also represent the way in which we present ourselves to the outside world. When the *wings* are particularly noticeable, attention is being drawn to our need for freedom or to the idea of how protective of ourselves we need to be.

THE SIGNIFICANCE

In dreams, from a mundane perspective, birds usually represent self-reliance and imagination. More esoterically, they have often been invested with magical and mystical powers, hence their appearance in many cultures as guides and mentors. Over the years they have also come to represent the soul – both its darker and its more enlightened side.

A bird flying freely represents our aspirations and desires and, *flying high*, the spirit set free and soaring towards the divine. The *golden-winged bird* has the same significance as fire and therefore indicates our spiritual, more esoteric aspirations. In a man's dream, a bird can represent awareness of his inner feminine. In a woman's dream, it is more likely to represent the archetypal self – that part of her being that has brought integration of her intuitive abilities.

THE SYMBOLISM OF BIRDS

This list helps us to gain a little understanding of how the symbology came about, how various qualities were ascribed to the birds and how they have developed as totems over the years.

BIRD	TOTEM MEANING	SYMBOLISM
Birds of prey	New vision	Dispassion, superiority
Carrion birds	The magic of creation	Bad luck, death
Cockerel	Sexuality	A new day, vigilance
Crow	Prophecy	Trickster
Cuckoo	Intuitive energy	Intrigue, perhaps cunning
Dove	Feminine energy	Tranquillity
Duck	Emotional comfort	Immaturity
Flamingo	Display of talents	Careful watchfulness

Game birds	Sacred movement	Chosen target, concealment
Gull	Ritual communication	Freedom, power
Hawk	Development of the psychic	Messenger
Ibis	Magical arts	The soul, perseverance
Jackdaw	Occult knowledge	Treachery, but also good news
Kingfisher	Boldness, opportunity	Honour, peaceful existence
Lark	Transcendence	Joy of creation
Magpie	Intelligence	Treachery, but also good news
Ostrich	Groundedness	Avoidance
Parrot	Mimicry	Gossip, loose talk
Peacock	Spiritual awakening	Understanding, rebirth
Pelican	Unselfishness	Nurturing
Penguin	Lucid dreaming, astral projection	Stability and yet fluidity

MYTHOLOGICAL, MAGICAL AND SPIRITUAL CREATURES

Given the opportunity, images of magical or mythical characters in our dreams allow us to access much forgotten knowledge. Mythology and the stories that surround the various *gods and goddesses* enable us to make sense of our own need for integration and understanding. When such figures appear in dreams they may appear as vengeful or helpful in turn. It does very much depend on the culture to which we belong as to which particular pantheon will resonate with us.

When we meet the *wizard, magician, priest, wise old man* or *guru* in our dreams, we are accessing the ancient arts of magic and alchemy. The magician might encourage us to explore high – or ceremonial – magic, the priest to explore our connection with the divine, the wise old man to study philosophy, and the guru to look at eastern religions.

When their feminine counterparts appear, we would do well to explore the more intuitive aspects of our beliefs. The *priestess*, for instance, might signify the commitment needed in practising the use of true intuition in our dealing with others. The conventional *witch with hat and broomstick,* however, would highlight the use of those powers in a slightly more flamboyant, perhaps less positive way.

Vampires and werewolves highlight the difficulty in integrating the two sides of our nature: good and evil, animal and human. Fear of the unknown, or of a darker force that appears to be life-threatening, is demonstrated when these creatures appear in dreams. Any *monster* appearing in a dream represents something that we have made larger than life.

THE SIGNIFICANCE

Myths and mythology, the collecting of those stories, are the external expression and embodiment of teachings that we have and will always require in order to find our own inner truth and innate power. Psychologically, when magic or magical elements appear in a dream, they are to do with our ability to link with our deepest powers. When we are using magic in a dream, we are using our energy to accomplish something without effort or difficulty. We are capable of controlling the situation that we are in, to have things happen for us and to create from our own needs and wants.

For a dreamer, night's the only time of day.

Bob Tzudiker and Noni White, *Newsies*

One can write, think and pray exclusively of others; dreams are all egocentric.

Evelyn Waugh

There are twelve hours in the day, and above fifty in the night.

Marie de Rabutin-Chantal

Don't fight with the pillow,
but lay down your head, and
kick every worriment out
of the bed.
Edmund Vance Cooke

BEHAVIOUR, ACTION AND ACTIVITY

In dreams, how we as dreamers and the characters in the dream scenario conduct themselves is pertinent to the overall interpretation of the dream. Specific actions will usually have specific meaning within a context and should be easily identifiable.

As an example, a dream character who is *waving* might be trying to attract our attention or to wave goodbye. If we are *being followed,* it might indicate that we are leading, being stalked or are forging ahead. *Being kissed* could be in greeting or as a sign of intimacy.

Physical activity in dreams is of particular note. When trying to gain information from what characters do, it is useful to categorize this into activity within a small space or that which entails movement to or from somewhere else. Thus, *washing your hands or getting up from a chair* belongs to the former, while *walking or running* to the latter. If the dream is to yield up all its secrets, we can pick up small details in this way.

Verbal and expressive communication are also relevant within dreams. *Whispering, calling, talking, shouting* and so on will all contain useful information in interpretation. Variously they show the need for privacy, to attract attention or disapproval. *Silence* when a question is asked, *a grunt, a frown or a shrug of the shoulders* all show varying degrees of disinterest. Within the framework of a dream, our emotions can be very different to those we have in everyday life. They may be more extreme, almost as though we have given ourselves freedom of expression. *A smile or a laugh, applause* or other expression of the connection between characters is always, therefore, worth acknowledging.

Ultimately, although they cannot necessarily be classed as actions, visual clues (seeing, noticing, recognizing etc), auditory and thinking activities all need to be acknowledged when understanding dreams. There is no actual imagery attached to them; they are simply experienced – there is an interaction that takes place.

THE SIGNIFICANCE

Our (or others') behaviour in a dream can differ markedly from normal, since the dream state gives us the freedom to highlight aspects of ourselves of which we would not normally be aware. Occasionally it is

therefore easier to ignore any symbology and simply work with the moods, feeling and emotions that have surfaced. Doing this will very often give us a clearer interpretation of our deeper sentiments.

By and large, what the dreamer is doing in a dream usually becomes self-evident and is fairly easily interpreted. What other dream characters are doing and how they are interacting with the dreamer or with one another equally needs to be assessed. That interaction may be positive in its outcome or negative. Ordinary everyday activities are just as significant as the more unusual; with a little experience in interpretation, they can add richness to the meaning.

Movement is also often relevant in dreams, particularly when it involves a change of location through our – or someone else's – activity. It will sometimes clarify our subsequent decisions in everyday life. *Crawling through a hole,* for instance, suggests that we can find a way through a difficulty, but only by adopting an effective, albeit uncomfortable, way of bypassing the difficulty.

Conversations, or any kind of verbal activity and communication, are also useful for interpreting what is being conveyed by the whole dream. Hearing and listening are an integral part of the interaction between people, so for these particular activities to be brought to our attention requires us to take careful note of what is going on. *Hearing* suggests registering a sound, speech or noise, whereas *listening* suggests absorbing the actual content of what is being heard.

We are often able to express clearly what we feel and think in dreams, whereas in waking life we may not feel confident enough to do so. The various characters may also express in their deeds or expressions what has not previously been apparent. *Thinking, feeling and assessing* as actual dream activities are also helpful in taking any action forward within the dream. These are usually activities carried out by the dreamer, and it may take a little time to get used to recognizing how that applies in the dream.

Laugh and the world laughs with you, snore and you sleep alone.

Anthony Burgess

There is no sunrise so beautiful that it is worth waking me up to see it.

Mindy Kaling

A day without a nap is like a cupcake without frosting.

Terri Guillemets

OCCUPATIONS

In dreams, fairytales and myths give us concepts of times past and modern-day occupations root us firmly in the present. Fixed in the here and now, occupations in dreams allow us points of contact with creativity and spirituality. As we progress through life, we come to realize that there is a huge store of knowledge that can be worked with to enhance our lives. People appearing in dreams are likely to have a particular significance for us depending on our upbringing and also our own way of working. It would not be unusual, for instance, for nurses and doctors to appear in a therapist's dreams. Here are some occupations and their better-known significances.

Performers and artists may serve in dreams as a projection of the type of person we would like to be. We may, for instance, in real life be shy and withdrawn, but need to be admired and loved. As a stereotype, such figures often represent our creative force and energy that encompasses more than simply artistic pursuits.

Music has a particularly beneficial healing effect. Any *musician,* therefore, could suggest a healer or therapist, but they could equally signify celebrity and our wish to be honoured. The figure of a *ballerina or dancer* often symbolizes our search for balance and poise, and can also suggest freedom and the joy of movement.

Dreaming of a *real estate agent,* or indeed anyone who is selling security in some way, epitomizes that part of us which needs a safe base from which to operate successfully in the world. The oppressive figure of a *bailiff or debt collector* usually represents a particular kind of authority figure.

A *doctor* in our dreams may suggest a known authority figure, and someone who has our best interests at heart. Such a figure may also represent a healing energy, in which case a *surgeon* would suggest the cutting out of something negative in our lives. We may in addition be in contact with our own inner *analyst or therapist.* Our instinctive knowledge of what is right for us will make itself known in dreams when, on a conscious level, we have

diverted from the correct path. Psychologically, the *chemist or pharmacist* represents the part of ourselves which is capable of making changes and is concerned about bodily health. By making calculated adjustments, a situation may be made more positive. An *osteopath* in dreams may suggest that part of us which is capable of manipulating the structure of our lives in order to achieve success, perhaps the release of trapped energy, to enable us to reach our full potential. Carers appearing in dreams suggest the more compassionate, nurturing side of ourselves. *Nurses or carers in the community* may suggest some kind of healing or specific act of palliative care. An *optician*, as someone who cares for the eyes of others, most often represents the need for clarity and wisdom, or rather knowledge specifically applied in our waking lives. It suggests the need to understand a situation that may be confusing us.

Traditionally, when an *alchemist* appears in dreams, something 'crude' or basic in our lives may be turned into something worthwhile. Such a figure may also represent ancient

or arcane knowledge. Dreaming of an *inventor* connects us with the more creative side of ourselves – someone who is capable of taking an idea and making it tangible.

THE SIGNIFICANCE

From the time that we are very small, we accept certain stereotypes as having relevance in our lives. Even characters in children's stories give a sense of the values and requirements of such occupations. As we mature, we give each occupation we encounter certain attributes that will often appear in our dreams.

Dreaming of *being at work* highlights issues, concerns or difficulties that we may have within the work situation. When we dream of working at something that does not have a place in our ordinary everyday lives, it may be worth exploring the potential within that line of work or its inherent qualities. We could be actively trying to make changes in our lives, or perhaps are having changes forced upon us through unemployment, redundancy or recession.

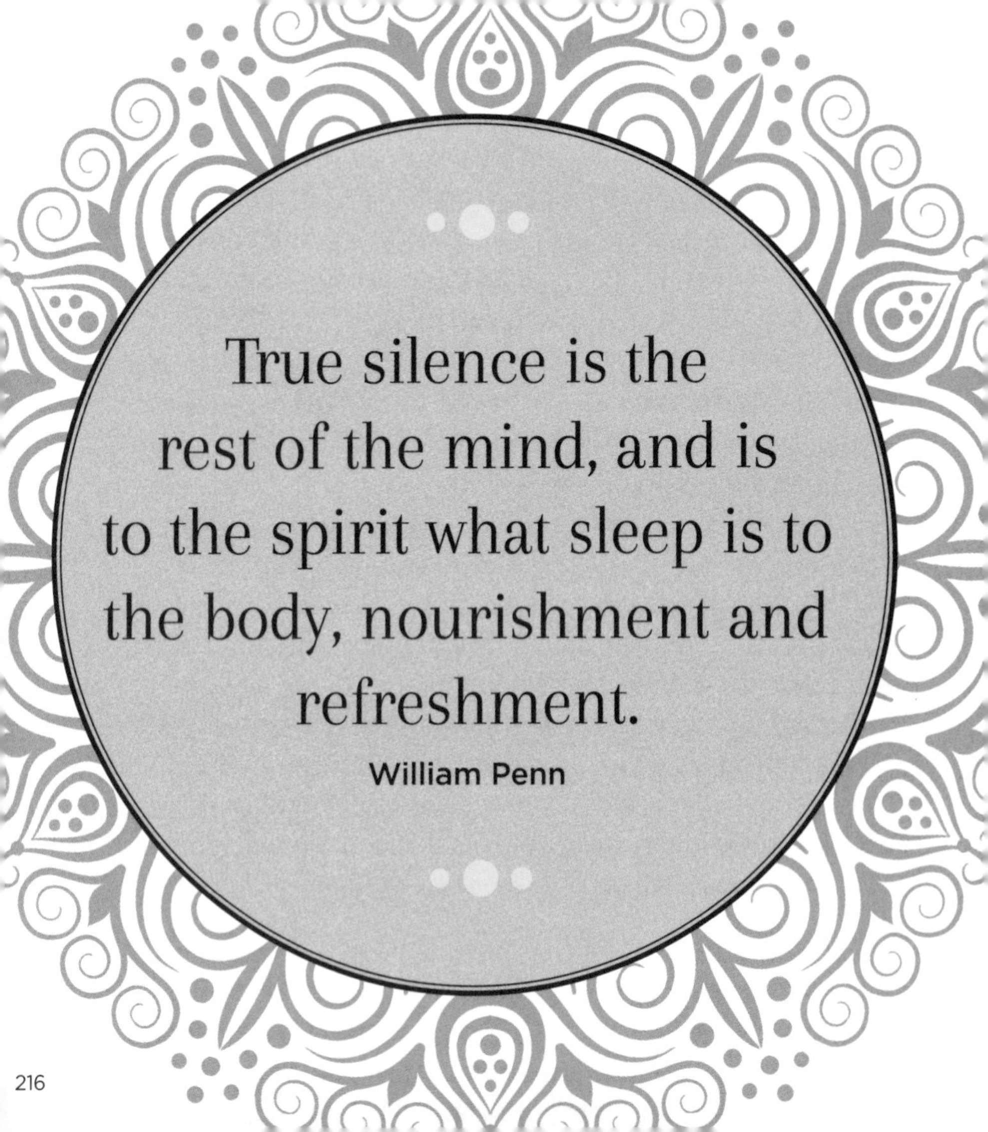

True silence is the rest of the mind, and is to the spirit what sleep is to the body, nourishment and refreshment.

William Penn

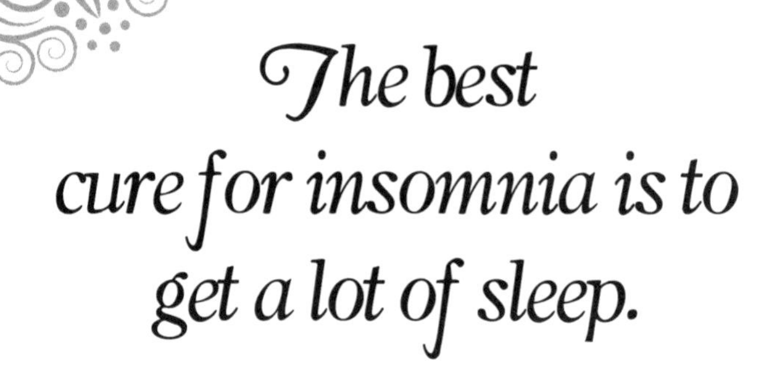

The best cure for insomnia is to get a lot of sleep.

W.C. Fields

EDUCATION

When we are relearning how to deal with the growth of our own personalities, the school or classroom will often begin to appear in our dreams.

Schools will often appear at times when we are attempting to get rid of old, outmoded ideas and concepts. When we are looking for guidance, it can be presented in dreams as a teacher. Often the figure will be that of a *headmaster, headmistress or professor* (someone who 'knows better').

A *lesson* is a previously planned form of instruction, the best and most efficient way that we can learn. It will very much have this meaning in dreams too. Dreaming of being in a *university* highlights our own individual potential and learning ability. Since a university is a place of higher learning, we are being made aware of the breadth of experience and increase in knowledge available to us. A *tutorial* implies one-to-one or small group teaching, so in the mundane sense will signify a need for us to understand specific ideas and concepts.

THE SIGNIFICANCE

School is an important part of everyone's life. If we are learning new abilities or skills in waking life, the image of a school will often come up in dreams. It is also the place where we experience associations that do not belong to the family, and can therefore suggest new ways of learning about relationships. We should also be considering our own need for discipline or disciplined action.

For many people, a teacher is the first figure of authority they meet outside the family. That person may have a profound effect, and the teacher is often dreamt about in later years. From any perspective, teaching is the passing on of information of things we need to know. Dreams are an efficient way of giving us such information, and with practice can be used effectively to help ourselves and others. Those teachings that we receive intuitively and in dreams have the greatest relevance to us as we progress on our journey.

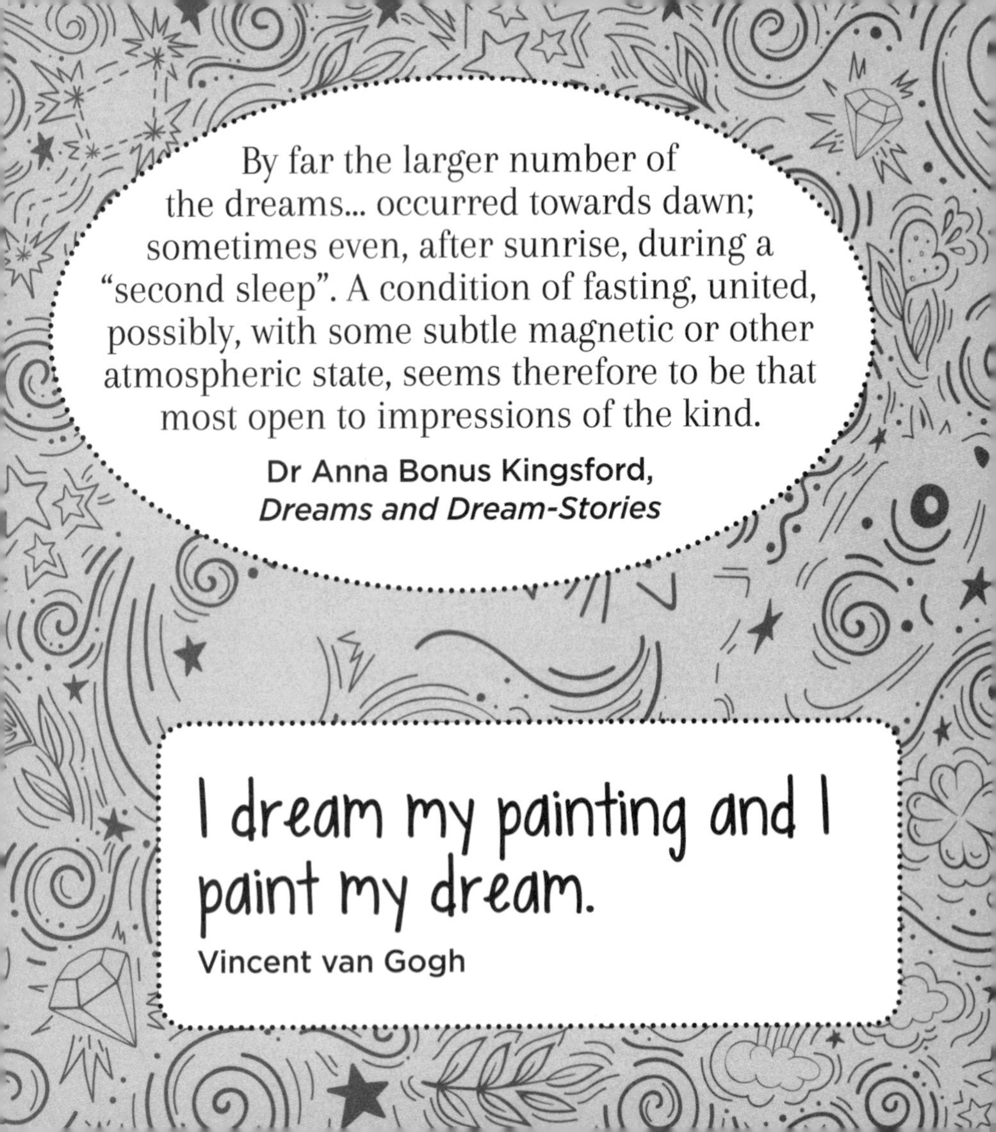

By far the larger number of the dreams... occurred towards dawn; sometimes even, after sunrise, during a "second sleep". A condition of fasting, united, possibly, with some subtle magnetic or other atmospheric state, seems therefore to be that most open to impressions of the kind.

Dr Anna Bonus Kingsford,
Dreams and Dream-Stories

I dream my painting and I paint my dream.

Vincent van Gogh

I like the night. Without the dark, we'd never see the stars.

Stephenie Meyer, *Twilight*

Be careful what you water your dreams with. Water them with worry and fear and you will produce weeds that choke the life from your dream. Water them with optimism and solutions and you will cultivate success. Always be on the lookout for ways to turn a problem into an opportunity for success. Always be on the lookout for ways to nurture your dream.

Lao Tzu

THE BODY

The body offers a great deal of material for interpretation. Its various systems – skeletal, circulatory, muscular – provide rich imagery that is reflected in every life.

Any *limb* can be taken to suggest the fears associated with gender issues and our core values. *Being dismembered* can be taken in its literal sense – we are being torn apart and need to restructure our lives and begin again.

More specifically, *legs* represent our personal means of support. If the *right leg* is highlighted, this suggests movement in a logical sense and may represent moving forward of our own volition, whereas the *left leg* tends to suggest passive movement, perhaps following someone else's lead.

In dreams, the *foot* can have several meanings. It can represent the way we make contact with reality, our sense of pragmatism. It can also suggest our ability to ground ourselves and our sense of stability.

Being aware of the *knees* in dreams again highlights the support we are able to give ourselves, this time from an emotional perspective. To be *on our knees* is symbolic of the requirement for prayer and entreaty, and perhaps our inability to move forward without help. *Someone else being on their knees* shows a level of emotional commitment, yet at the same time may also represent an act of submission. The *heel* symbolizes that part of ourselves which is strong and supportive but, at the same time, can be vulnerable. *A winged ankle or foot* suggests a need for a different, more efficient form of expression. To be *grinding the heel into the ground* in dreams suggests determination or anger.

Generally, *arms* signify our ability to love, or to give and take. Depending on the position of the arms, we may also be indicating supplication or showing passionate commitment. The *hands* are two of the most expressive parts of the body, and signify power and creativity. See the chart on pages 228–9 to see what the different gestures mean.

When the dream appears to concentrate on the *abdomen,* there is a need for us to focus on our emotions and repressed feelings. We may need to look at how we protect ourselves from other people's negativity in waking life. When we become conscious of our own or someone else's *bottom,* this may be a play on words in that we have literally 'reached the bottom' of issues. Often in dreams, the mind returns to the initial childlike gaining control of bodily functions, particularly that of evacuation. This control is the beginning of self-realization, self-reliance and control, yet at the same time of suppression and defence. Any evacuation of the *bowel* highlights our need to be free of worry; excrement in dreams interestingly enough can highlight financial anxieties. In its more esoteric meaning, it belongs to the realm of feelings. We may simply be trying to get rid of bad feelings that can ultimately be turned into something more worthwhile.

THE SIGNIFICANCE

The body forms the prime source of information about us, and often highlights problems we may have. Psychological stress translated into bodily images often becomes a fertile source of symbolism. When emotions cannot be faced in everyday life, they very often appear as distorted body images in dreams.

The *head* is the principal part of the body – the motivating force. As the seat of intellect, it denotes power and wisdom. Dreaming of the head suggests that we should consider very carefully how we handle both intelligence and foolishness. To dream of the *head being bowed* suggests prayer, invocation or supplication. When the *head is covered* it shows we may be hiding our own intelligence, or perhaps acknowledging somebody else's superiority. A *blow to the head* in a dream indicates that we should reconsider our actions in waking life.

The *hair* represents strength and virility. To be *having our hair cut* suggests that we are trying to create order in our lives. In dreams, to be *combing or brushing* the hair, either our own or someone else's, is to be attempting to untangle a particular attitude prevalent in our lives. To be *cutting someone else's hair* suggests that we may be curtailing a particular activity. To be *bald* in a dream rather than in waking life shows that we are recognizing our own innate intelligence or wisdom.

Any dream where the *eye* is noticeable is connected with our powers of observation and the ability to be discriminating. The eye is connected with the power of light and, in ancient times, to the sun gods, when it often became a talisman representing perception. *Loss of eyesight* in dreams suggests loss of clarity in waking life; the loss of logic (right eye) or loss of intuition (left eye). *Regaining the eyesight* can indicate a return to innocence and clear-sightedness.

Representing our need to express ourselves, the *mouth* in dreams will often help us to decide how best to handle a situation in waking life. If the mouth appears to be *shouting*, forceful action is required; if *whispering*, a more gentle approach is needed. Dreams of *teeth* are perhaps one of the commonest universal dreams. In old-style interpretation, they were thought to stand for aggressive sexuality, though it is perhaps more appropriate to recognize that, as the teeth are the first visible change in a baby, they represent transition periods in our lives. Teeth falling or coming out easily in dreams mean such a transition is on the horizon.

The *jaw* depicts our way of expressing ourselves. *Pain in the jaw* in dreams can signify our need to release some kind of tension in our lives, possibly by expressing ourselves more fully. When we become aware of the *throat* in dreams, we are conscious of the need for self-expression and perhaps of our own vulnerability. The *tongue* is associated with our understanding of information that we wish to pass on to other people; a *forked tongue* can suggest duplicity. The *nose* in dreams can often stand for curiosity, and also for intuition. A proportionately *large nose* can indicate we feel that someone is interfering in our lives, whereas a *small nose* may suggest a degree of disinterest.

SYMBOLISM OF HANDS

Gesture has always been an important part of communication, which is why the hands in dreams convey so much meaning without the need for words. Here are some of the meanings of different hand gestures.

IMAGE	MEANING
Clenched fist	A threat
Folded hands	A state of rest or deep peace
Hands covering the eyes	Shame, fear or horror
Hands on the head	Thought and care are necessary
Hands placed in someone else's hands	Surrender
Hands raised towards the sky	Adoration or prayer

Left hand	Passivity and receptiveness
Open hand	Justice
Hands placed together as if in prayer	Defencelessness or supplication
Pointing finger	A way forward
Right hand	Power and energy
Thumb pointing downwards	Adverse energy
Thumb pointing upwards	Power, beneficial energy
Two hands noticeably different	Conflict between belief and feeling
Two people's hands clasped	Union or friendship
Washing of hands (ours or others)	Rejection of guilt or awareness of difficulties
Wringing hands	Grief and distress

I honor health as the first muse, and sleep as the condition of health. Sleep benefits mainly by the sound health it produces; incidentally also by dreams, into whose farrago a divine lesson is sometimes slipped.

Ralph Waldo Emerson, *Letters and Social Aims, "Inspiration"*

You know that place between sleep and awake, that place where you still remember dreaming? That's where I'll always love you. That's where I'll be waiting.

James V. Hart, *Hook*

Without leaps of imagination or dreaming, we lose the excitement of possibilities. Dreaming, after all is a form of planning.

Gloria Steinem

I love the silent hour of night,
For blissful dreams may then arise,
Revealing to my charmed sight
What may not bless my waking eyes.

Anne Brontë

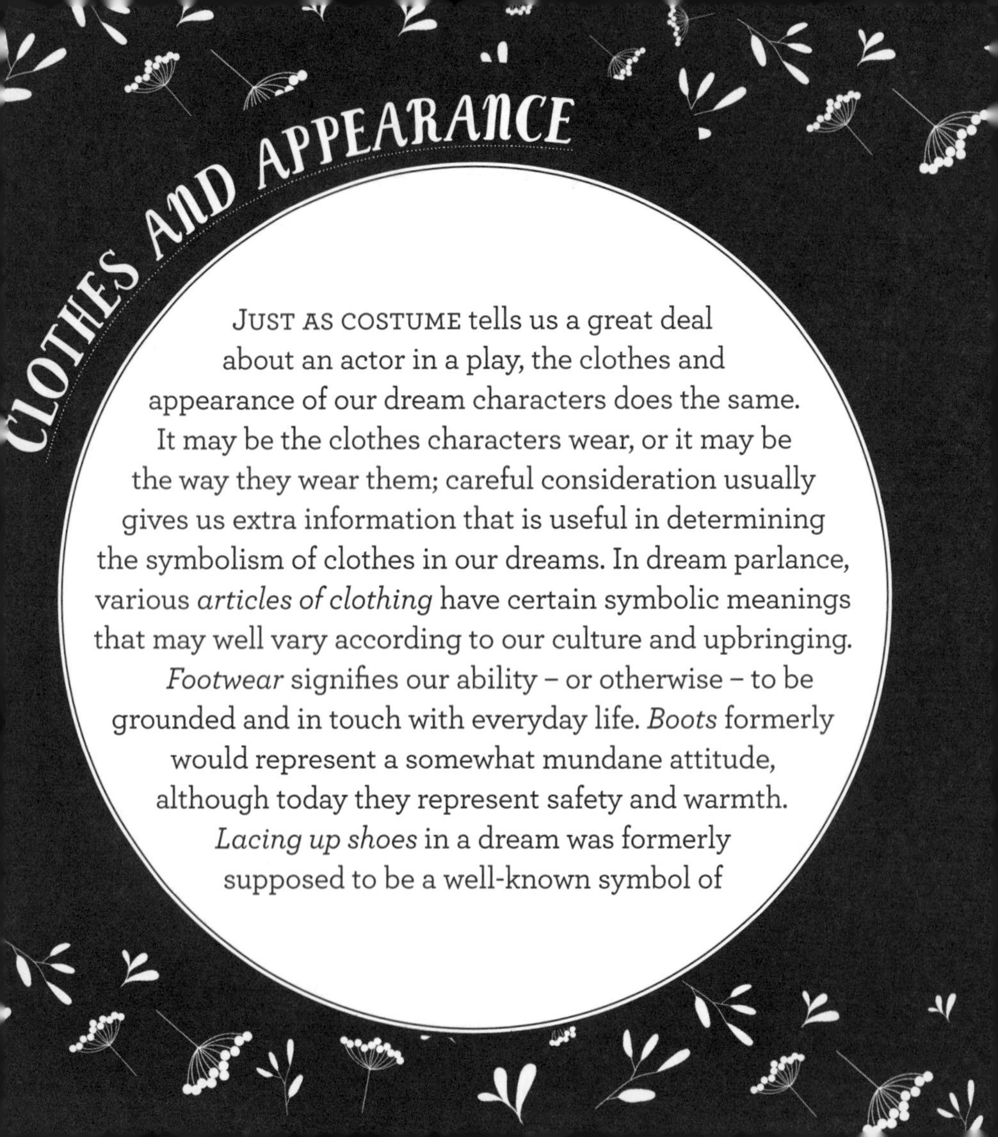

Clothes and Appearance

Just as costume tells us a great deal about an actor in a play, the clothes and appearance of our dream characters does the same. It may be the clothes characters wear, or it may be the way they wear them; careful consideration usually gives us extra information that is useful in determining the symbolism of clothes in our dreams. In dream parlance, various *articles of clothing* have certain symbolic meanings that may well vary according to our culture and upbringing.

Footwear signifies our ability – or otherwise – to be grounded and in touch with everyday life. *Boots* formerly would represent a somewhat mundane attitude, although today they represent safety and warmth. *Lacing up shoes* in a dream was formerly supposed to be a well-known symbol of

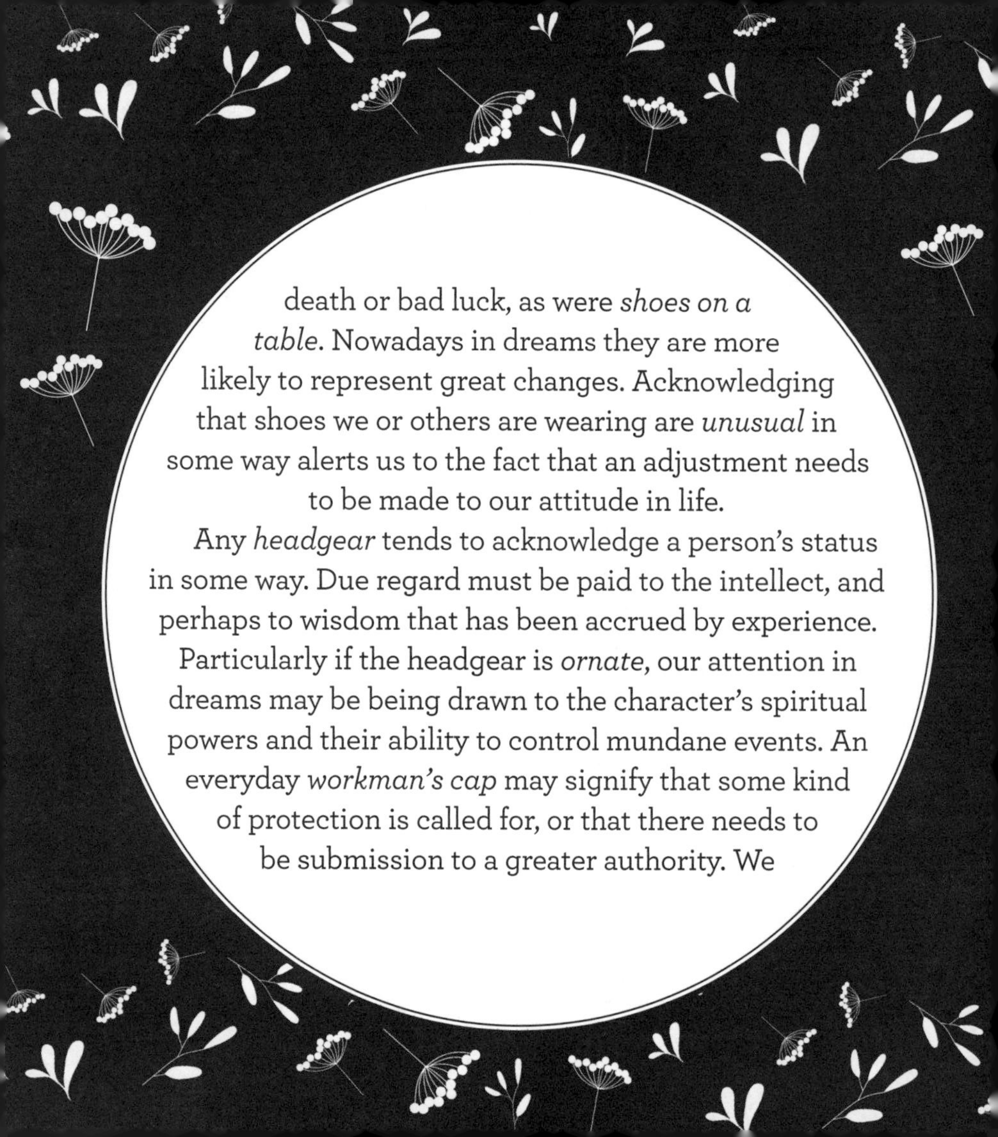

death or bad luck, as were *shoes on a table*. Nowadays in dreams they are more likely to represent great changes. Acknowledging that shoes we or others are wearing are *unusual* in some way alerts us to the fact that an adjustment needs to be made to our attitude in life.

Any *headgear* tends to acknowledge a person's status in some way. Due regard must be paid to the intellect, and perhaps to wisdom that has been accrued by experience. Particularly if the headgear is *ornate*, our attention in dreams may be being drawn to the character's spiritual powers and their ability to control mundane events. An everyday *workman's cap* may signify that some kind of protection is called for, or that there needs to be submission to a greater authority. We

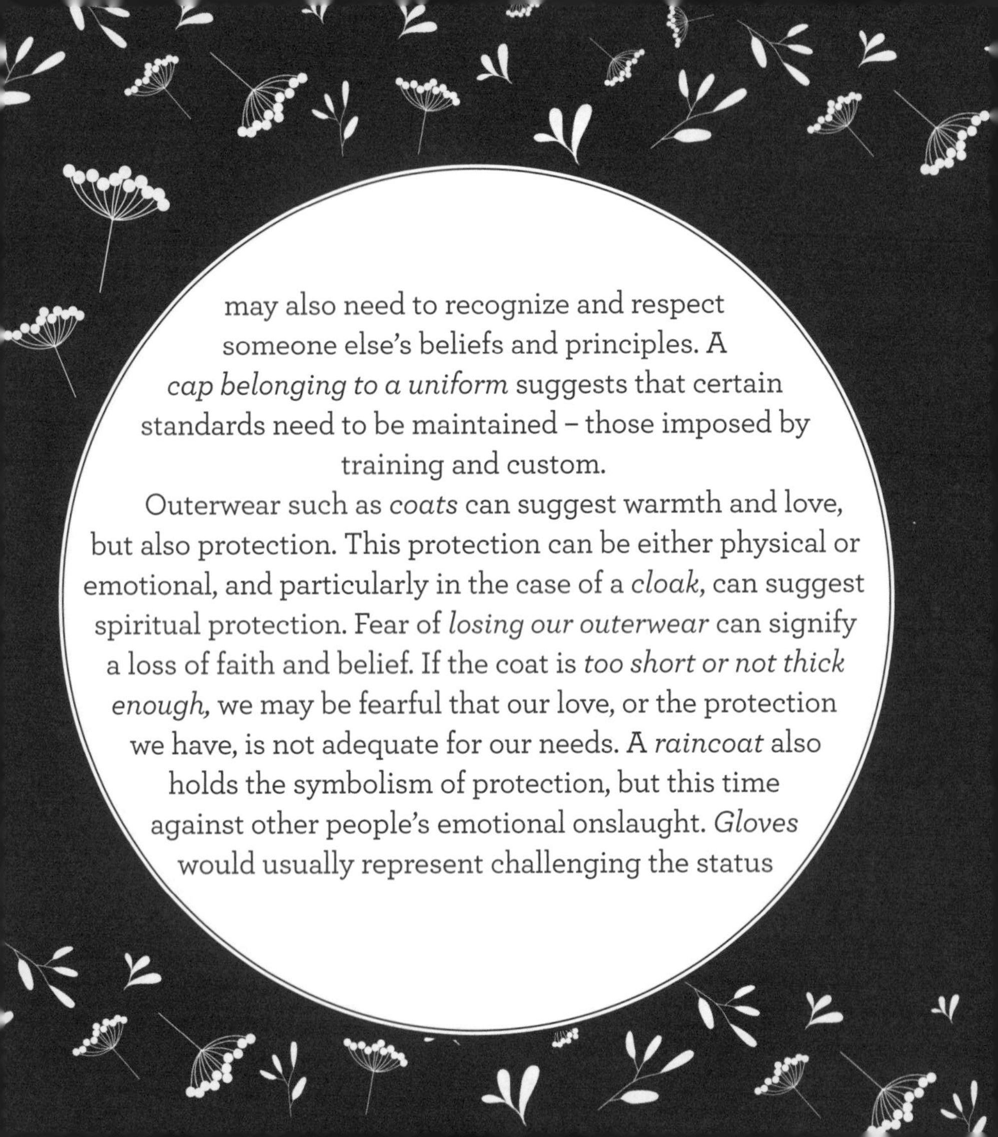

may also need to recognize and respect someone else's beliefs and principles. A *cap belonging to a uniform* suggests that certain standards need to be maintained – those imposed by training and custom.

Outerwear such as *coats* can suggest warmth and love, but also protection. This protection can be either physical or emotional, and particularly in the case of a *cloak*, can suggest spiritual protection. Fear of *losing our outerwear* can signify a loss of faith and belief. If the coat is *too short or not thick enough,* we may be fearful that our love, or the protection we have, is not adequate for our needs. A *raincoat* also holds the symbolism of protection, but this time against other people's emotional onslaught. *Gloves* would usually represent challenging the status

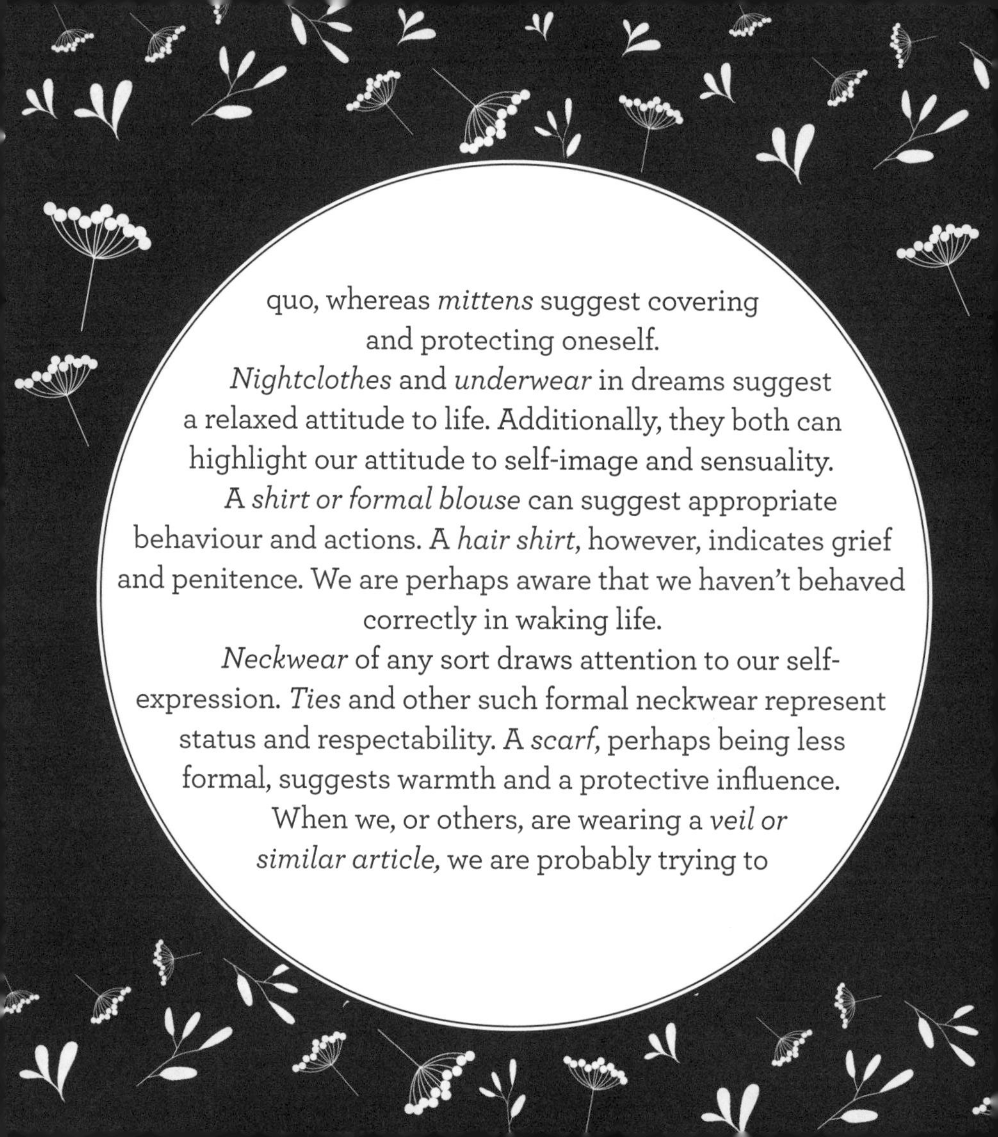

quo, whereas *mittens* suggest covering and protecting oneself.

Nightclothes and *underwear* in dreams suggest a relaxed attitude to life. Additionally, they both can highlight our attitude to self-image and sensuality.

A *shirt or formal blouse* can suggest appropriate behaviour and actions. A *hair shirt*, however, indicates grief and penitence. We are perhaps aware that we haven't behaved correctly in waking life.

Neckwear of any sort draws attention to our self-expression. *Ties* and other such formal neckwear represent status and respectability. A *scarf*, perhaps being less formal, suggests warmth and a protective influence.

When we, or others, are wearing a *veil or similar article,* we are probably trying to

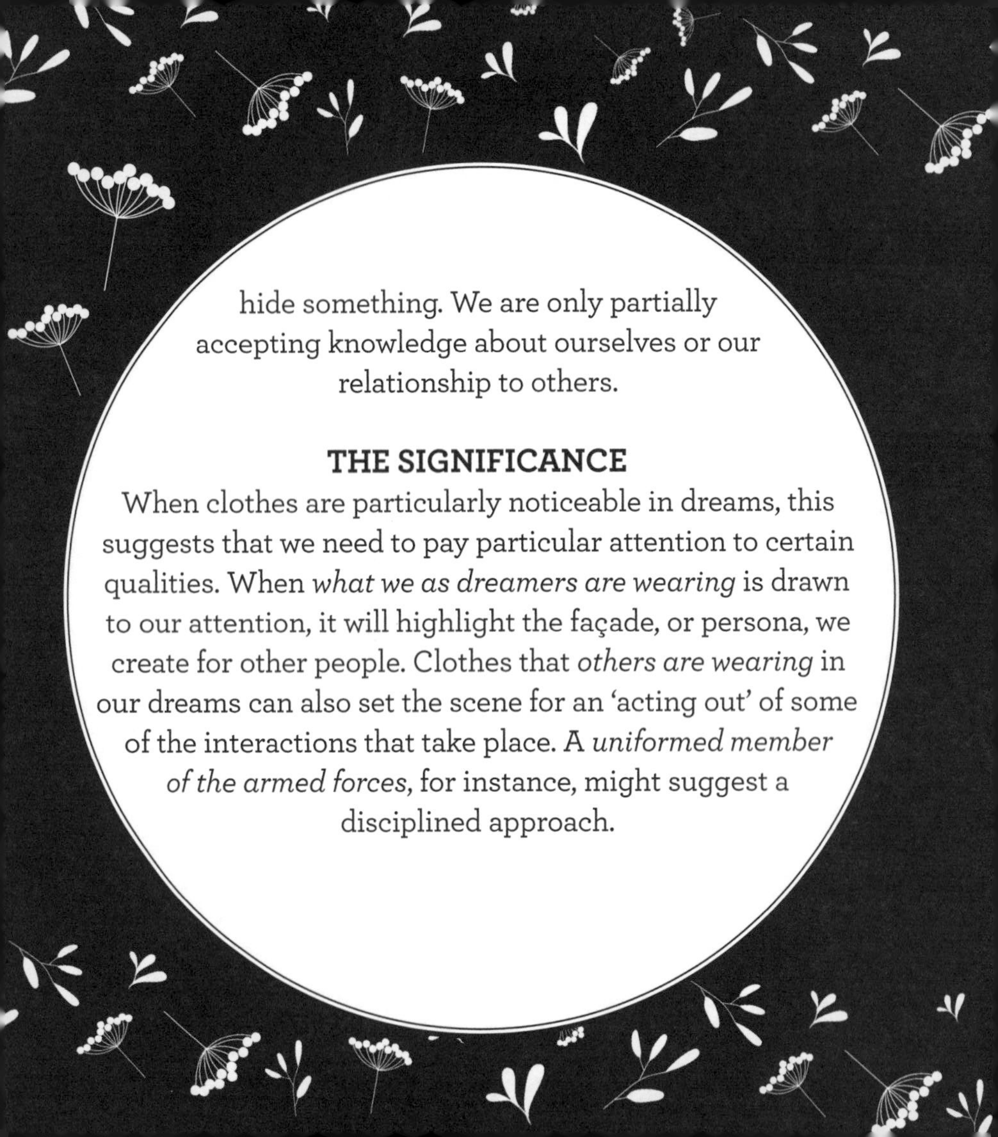

hide something. We are only partially accepting knowledge about ourselves or our relationship to others.

THE SIGNIFICANCE

When clothes are particularly noticeable in dreams, this suggests that we need to pay particular attention to certain qualities. When *what we as dreamers are wearing* is drawn to our attention, it will highlight the façade, or persona, we create for other people. Clothes that *others are wearing* in our dreams can also set the scene for an 'acting out' of some of the interactions that take place. A *uniformed member of the armed forces,* for instance, might suggest a disciplined approach.

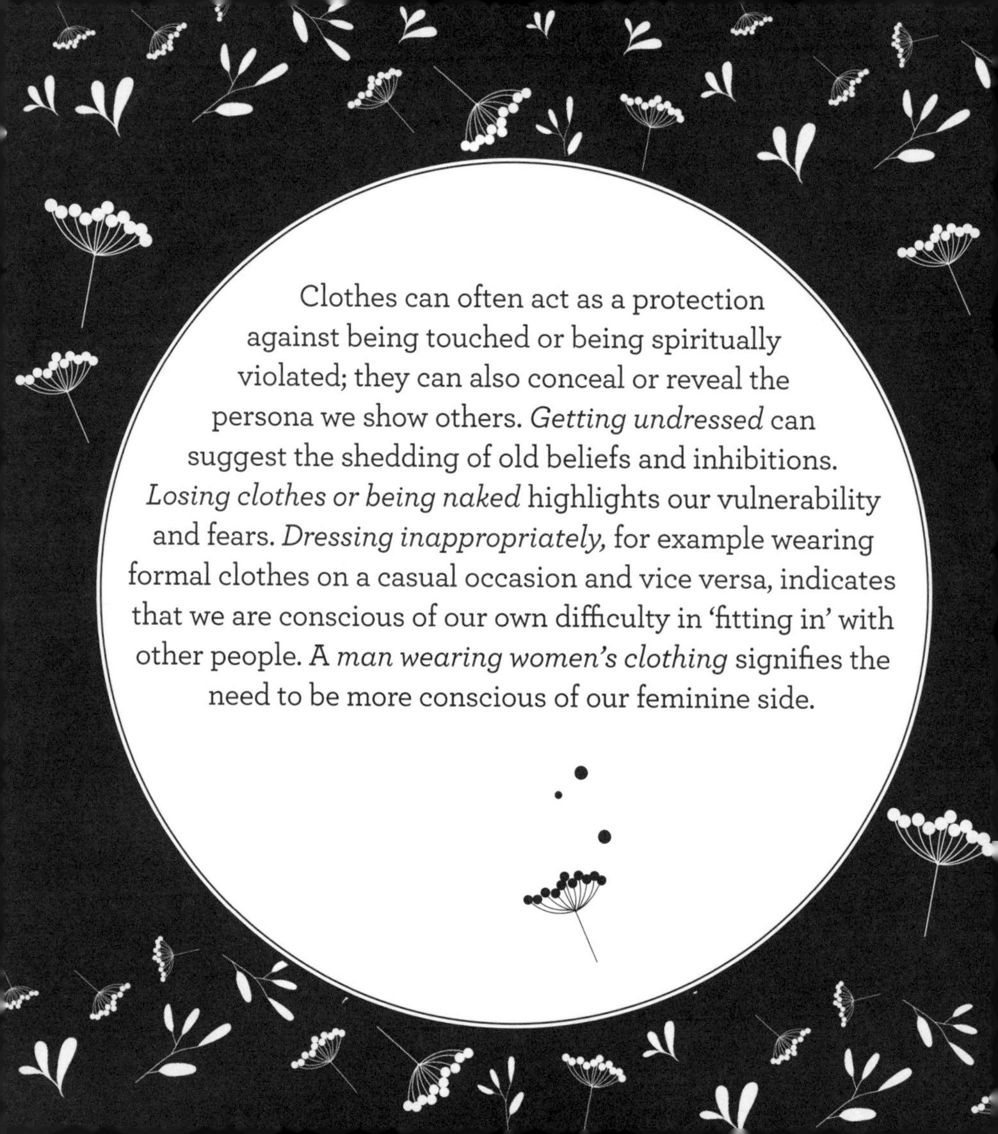

Clothes can often act as a protection against being touched or being spiritually violated; they can also conceal or reveal the persona we show others. *Getting undressed* can suggest the shedding of old beliefs and inhibitions. *Losing clothes or being naked* highlights our vulnerability and fears. *Dressing inappropriately,* for example wearing formal clothes on a casual occasion and vice versa, indicates that we are conscious of our own difficulty in 'fitting in' with other people. A *man wearing women's clothing* signifies the need to be more conscious of our feminine side.

POSITIVE INTERACTIONS AND CELEBRATIONS

The way we feel in our dreams, and the way we react to other people in them, can tell us much about how we are perceived. Positive relationships in dreams can underscore the joy we feel in our everyday lives as we enjoy friendship, love and interacting with like-minded people. We can learn about trust in our dealings with others, and about our attitude to sensuality.

Positive interactions, sometimes quantified as friendliness, are by and large a deliberate and purposeful action by one character towards another. This might include: *kissing* or other physical activity such as *shaking hands; sharing a pleasant*

activity; helping or being helped by a dream character; giving someone a present or gift; acknowledging someone's presence; or having kindly thoughts or feelings about another character.

Being with other people, whether in a group or otherwise, is often a measure of our maturity and how we handle our public persona. In dreams, a *banquet, party* or any *celebration meal* is a symbol for the joy of being in the company of others like ourselves, and perhaps for mutual nourishment.

Festivals and carnivals were initially a time when the gods and powers of nature were thanked and propitiated in order to ensure a good harvest. In dreams, the important aspect of both secular festivals and carnivals is to suggest that we can drop our inhibitions and allow ourselves the freedom to express ourselves fully. A *holiday* – quite literally, the word means 'holy-day' – is time set apart when we take the opportunity to create space for

ourselves, and often has this meaning in dreams. To dream of a *public holiday* can indicate that we are part of a more relaxed way of being.

THE SIGNIFICANCE

Behaviour in dreams is highly significant, giving many clues about the way in which we need to make an interpretation. There are two ways to look at what is called positive interaction as part of behaviour in dreams. The first is that instigated by us as dreamer, and the second is that initiated by other dream characters. In the first instance, we will wish to interpret our own motives and what we felt. In the second, we will look at our own reaction and response to the other's actions.

Using touch as an example, our interpretations will depend on these considerations. *Touch* in dreams suggests making

contact. We – or they – are linking with others, usually to our mutual advantage. Touch in a positive way is usually an act of appreciation and approval.

Giving is one of the fundamental needs of human beings; this need is often echoed in dreams. To be able to *share* represents our ability to interact with others, to have others belong within our lives and to assume responsibility for them. *Being given something* in a dream may signify that we are being given information or knowledge, perhaps to share with others and to create an environment that allows for give and take.

And if tonight my soul may find her peace
in sleep, and sink in good oblivion,
and in the morning wake like a new-opened flower
then I have been dipped again in God, and new-created.

D.H. Lawrence

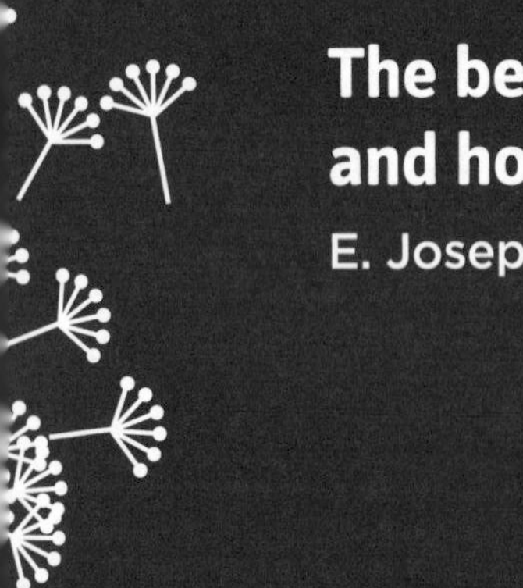

The best bridge between despair and hope is a good night's sleep.

E. Joseph Cossman

There is more refreshment and stimulation in a nap, even of the briefest, than in all the alcohol ever distilled.

Edward Lucas

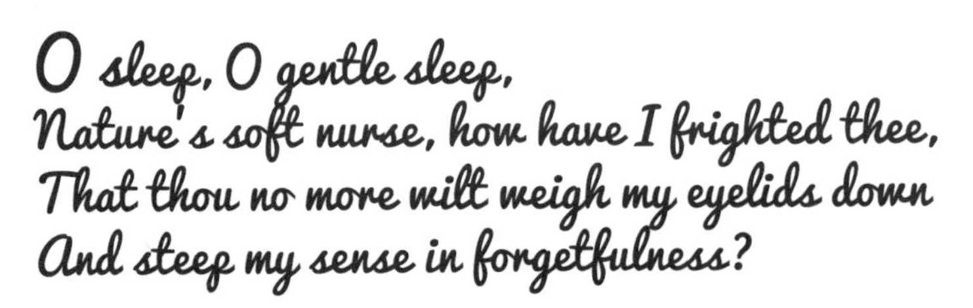

O sleep, O gentle sleep,
Nature's soft nurse, how have I frighted thee,
That thou no more wilt weigh my eyelids down
And steep my sense in forgetfulness?

William Shakespeare, *Henry IV, Part I*

NEGATIVE ACTIONS AND INTERACTIONS

CONFLICT SITUATIONS CAN appear in our dreams, either physical or emotional, and these can highlight our own negative behaviour, or that of others, or our own vulnerability. Negativity in dreams is usually related to something that is out of kilter in our waking lives: potential danger, bad behaviour or perhaps emotional issues.

Dreams can often point to a danger in symbolic form, such as *conflict of any sort, fire or flood*. It may be that someone has uncovered a vulnerability within us that we now have an opportunity to deal with, or perhaps that our dreams highlight our own *bad behaviour* or that of others. *Stealing or thieving*

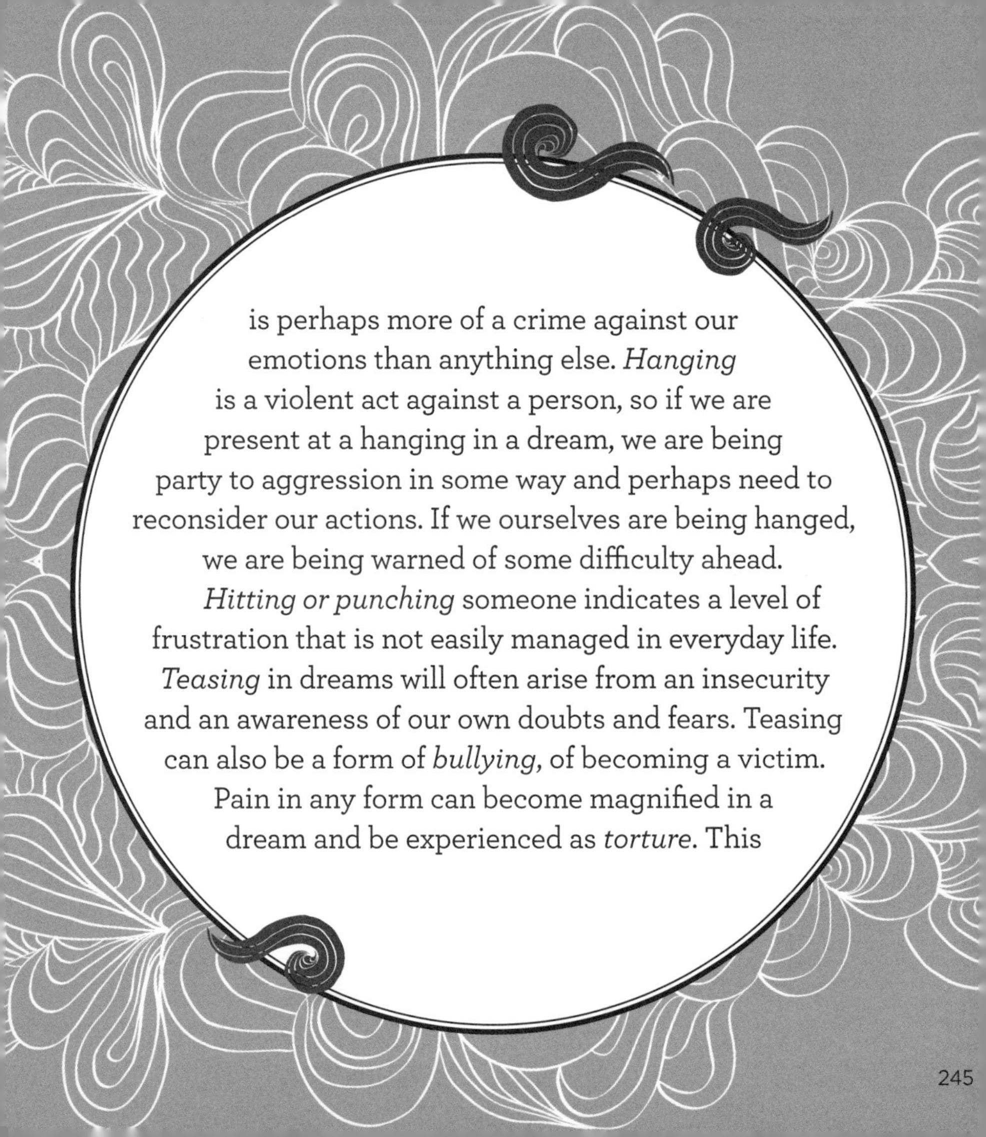

is perhaps more of a crime against our emotions than anything else. *Hanging* is a violent act against a person, so if we are present at a hanging in a dream, we are being party to aggression in some way and perhaps need to reconsider our actions. If we ourselves are being hanged, we are being warned of some difficulty ahead.

Hitting or punching someone indicates a level of frustration that is not easily managed in everyday life. *Teasing* in dreams will often arise from an insecurity and an awareness of our own doubts and fears. Teasing can also be a form of *bullying*, of becoming a victim. Pain in any form can become magnified in a dream and be experienced as *torture*. This

magnification is designed by the dreamer to highlight a problem in waking life that needs dealing with immediately.

THE SIGNIFICANCE

Negative actions and interactions are as much an essential aspect of understanding dreams as positive ones. Any aggressive act is highly threatening to the status quo, and even less obviously negative acts, such as *turning away* from someone, can be meaningful. *Obsessive or repetitive behaviour* in dreams often occurs in order to ensure that we have fully understood the message being conveyed by the unconscious. An emotional difficulty in waking life can be upsetting, and

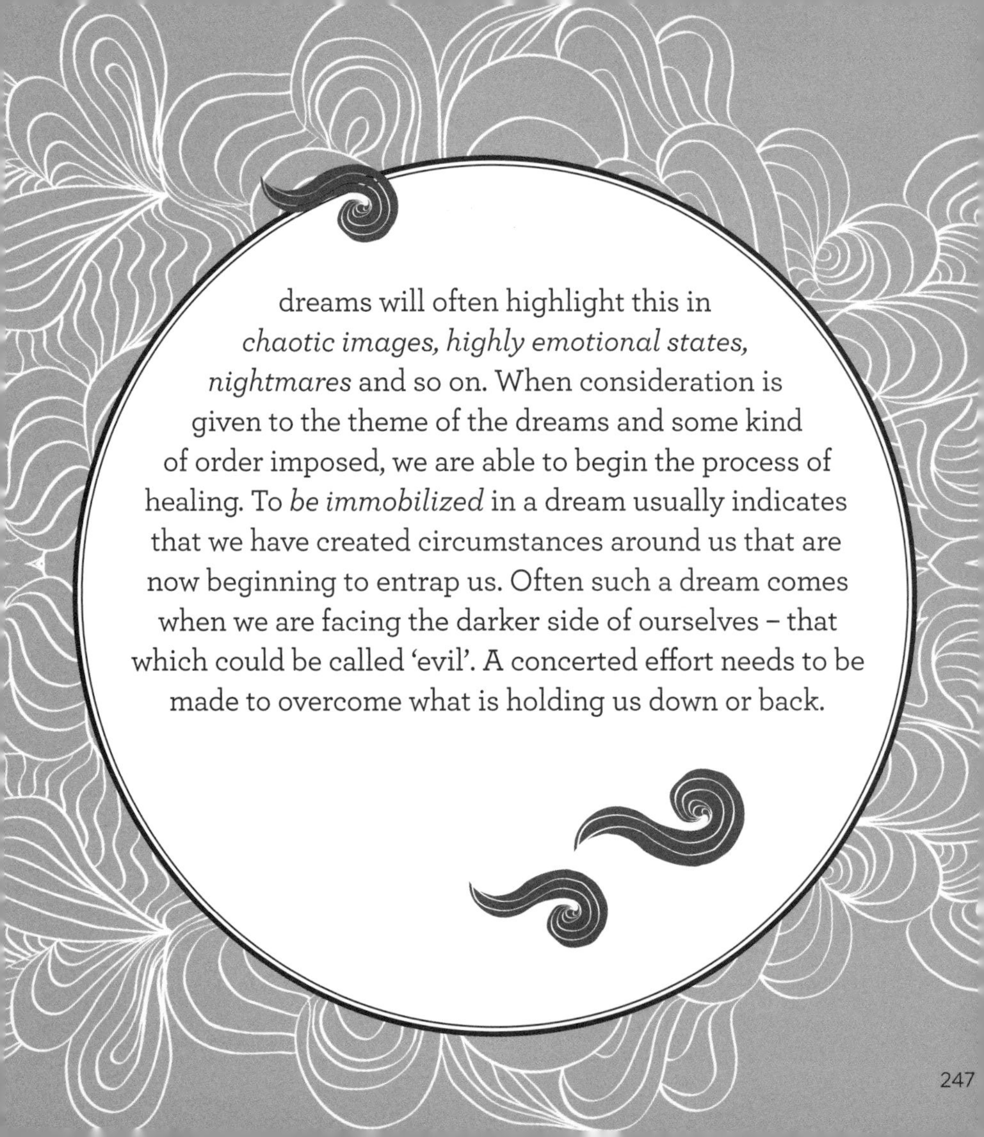

dreams will often highlight this in *chaotic images, highly emotional states, nightmares* and so on. When consideration is given to the theme of the dreams and some kind of order imposed, we are able to begin the process of healing. To *be immobilized* in a dream usually indicates that we have created circumstances around us that are now beginning to entrap us. Often such a dream comes when we are facing the darker side of ourselves – that which could be called 'evil'. A concerted effort needs to be made to overcome what is holding us down or back.

RELATIONSHIPS AND INTIMACY

Dreams can shed light on all aspects of our sensual and sexual natures, on our relationships with others and on our need for contact, both physical and emotional.

One vital stage of growth in a baby's development is its fascination with its own body and the ability to be physical and sensual. This has much to do with how it feels to be in one's own skin, as it were. It is at this point that he or she learns about touch and approval from other people, about whether it is nice to touch or be touched, and even if sensuality is appropriate. This is the growth of *trust*, and in any relationship, whether intimate or otherwise, this is an important part of our awareness of our essential being.

When there is, or has been, difficulty in this area, while any original trauma may be suppressed in waking life, it will often surface in dreams when the time is right for it to be dealt with. Real progress takes place when we are not afraid of the curiosity that allows an innocent exploration of our own bodies and that of others.

One essential aspect of dreaming is the appreciation and feedback we receive from our dream characters. Learning from this interaction, relating to other people in the waking world then runs the whole gamut of relationships, from trusting our own reactions and our ability to communicate, to more intimate behaviour.

Within ourselves we hold both masculine and feminine potentials. Various aspects of sex and sexuality can appear in dreams, as much in explanation of our unique drives and intuition as actual need for intimacy. One potential is always more overt than the other;

there is often conflict between the inner and the outer expression of these. This conflict can sometimes show itself in dreams as apparent *bisexuality* and a need for a positive relationship with members of both sexes.

In dreams, *transexualism and transvestism* signify a fluidity as far as gender roles are concerned. Dreaming of a *hermaphrodite* (someone who is both masculine and feminine) suggests a degree of androgyny – the perfect balance within one person of the masculine and feminine qualities.

Often when there are issues to do with confidence, the image of *castration* will appear in a dream. Its appearance suggests that we fear the loss of drive and masculinity as well as sexual power. To be *castrating someone* suggests an act of disempowerment. Dreaming of *contraception* can indicate a fear of pregnancy and birth, although interestingly it can equally indicate the choices we make when taking responsibility for our own bodies and actions.

The conflicts that arise in us because of our physical desire for someone can be dealt with in the dream state through dreaming of *sex*. Dreams actually have an odd way of manifesting images of primitive rites and practices of which we may have no conscious knowledge. Many of these are representations of intimacy.

In dreams, a *kiss* can indicate either a mark of respect or an innate desire to waken that part of us represented by the dream partner. The wish or need to be able to communicate with someone on a very close level can also translate itself into *sexual intimacy* in a dream. Often such an act really marks the integration of a particular part of our own personality.

THE SIGNIFICANCE

Any interaction between dream characters or ourselves as dreamers reflects, to a large extent, our feelings about ourselves and the world in which we live. If the characters are *known to us* in waking life or we have a sense in the dream that we *already know them*, then we might learn a great deal about our own reactions by looking at what they do *to* us (passivity), what they do *for* us (positivity), and what the outcome (probability) might be. This gives us an awareness of another part of our personality that can be integrated into our overall persona. A relationship in that sense is not based purely on male/female intimacy, but is really the marrying together of two aspects. This is often seen in dreams as an actual *marriage ceremony*.

Sexuality in a dream, in the sense of *feeling desire for someone else*, is a basic biological urge for closeness and/or union with what that person represents. We are perhaps searching for a part of ourselves that we have lost. The character to whom we feel linked represents the closest we can get to that part. If we had reached a state of full integration, we would presumably have no need for sexual union with someone else. However, most of us have a desire to be at one with everything that is not part of our own ego.

Such a sensual dream, which highlights the feelings we are capable of having, provides information that enables us to understand our own needs. Sexual activity in waking life might be seen as either the highest expression of love and spirituality, or if purely physically based, entirely selfish. In spiritual terms, each of us is searching for a union, a conjoining of all aspects of ourselves, and this will often be depicted in dreams.

Equally, as we mature spiritually, we must sometimes

undertake tasks and actions that are not always understood by others. If we find ourselves unpopular in our dreams, we must decide whether our own code of conduct is right for us or whether, in fact, we are acting for the greater good. Dreaming of being alone highlights being single, isolated or lonely. More positively, it represents the need for independence. As we have said in relation to belonging to a group, loneliness can be experienced as a negative state, whereas being alone is different, and can be very positive.

Always wear cute pyjamas to bed, you'll never know who you will meet in your dreams.

Joel Madden

It seems that everyone has their own inexplicable fear to have nightmares about. We need nightmares to keep ourselves entertained, and fend off the contentment that we all fear and abhor so much.

Louis de Bernières

Nights through dreams tell the myths forgotten by the day.

Carl Jung, *Memories, Dreams, Reflections*

Man is a genius when he is dreaming.

Akira Kurosawa

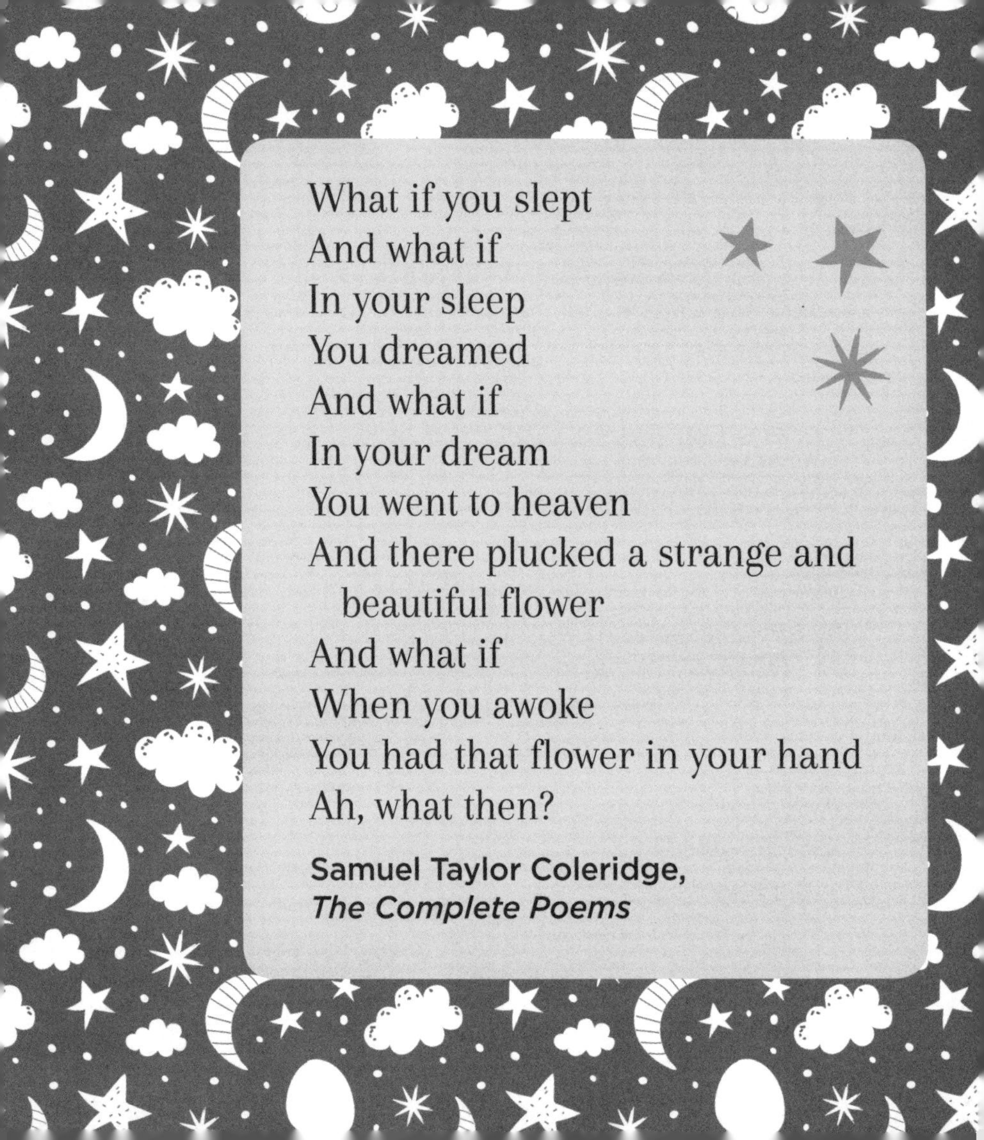
What if you slept
And what if
In your sleep
You dreamed
And what if
In your dream
You went to heaven
And there plucked a strange and
beautiful flower
And what if
When you awoke
You had that flower in your hand
Ah, what then?

Samuel Taylor Coleridge,
The Complete Poems

FOOD AND DRINK

Whether physical, mental or spiritual, food and drink signify a satisfaction of our needs. Frequent dreams about eating suggest a hunger for something, not necessarily food.

Bread is symbolic of life itself. It is said to be 'food for the soul' and can also represent the need to share, particularly if it appears in dreams in celebratory meals. Depending on whether we are *eating alone or in a group, meals* can indicate acceptance and sociability. When we are *baking* and making cakes, it indicates our need to care for others or to nurture an inner, perhaps hidden, need within ourselves. *Cake* itself signifies sensual enjoyment of several sorts. *Sweets and chocolate* in dreams tend to represent sensual pleasures. As a healing substance, *honey* has the power to regenerate the essence of our feelings; more esoterically it symbolizes immortality and rebirth. *Like honey, jam* will normally signify an additional sweetness or flavour to life. In the sense of *preserving fruit* for future use, jam also symbolizes harvesting with awareness. When *fruits or berries* appear in dreams, we are representing in dream form the fruits of our experience or effort, and the potential for prosperity.

Physical or worldly satisfaction or needs are often shown in dreams as *meat,* although *raw meat* can supposedly signify impending misfortune. *Fish,* on the other hand, symbolizes temporal and spiritual power. Dreaming of fish connects with the emotional side of ourselves, as well as with our ability to be wise without necessarily being strategic. *Vegetables* represent our basic needs and material satisfaction. They may also symbolize the benefits we gain from the earth and situations around us. Interestingly, the different layers and facets of our personality are often shown as an *onion.*

As an easily obtainable drink and one of our first experiences in infancy, *milk* signifies nourishment of the inner self.

THE SIGNIFICANCE

Our need – or enjoyment – of food in waking life fulfils certain psychological needs, and its appearance in dreams will highlight those requirements. Dreaming of *eating* shows that we are attempting to satisfy our deepest wants or hunger; it may be that we lack some basic nutrient or feedback in our lives. To *not eat or refuse food* indicates an avoidance of growth and change. We may be attempting to isolate ourselves from others or be in conflict with ourselves over our body image. *Cooking* can symbolize creativity or nurturing a new skill or ability of any type. To be able to move forward in our lives, we may need to blend certain parts of our existence in new and original ways in order to succeed.

Drinking anything at all in a dream may indicate our need for comfort and sustenance, to be absorbing or taking something in. It symbolizes the interplay between the inner need to sustain life and the external availability of nourishment. The refusal by someone in a dream to give you water can mean that an important person in your life – often a parent – is withholding emotional support, in order to punish some real or imagined infraction.

If you refuse someone water, it can indicate that you are being asked to make a commitment that you feel is too demanding of your time and energy.

A good laugh and a long sleep are the best cures in the doctor's book.

Irish proverb

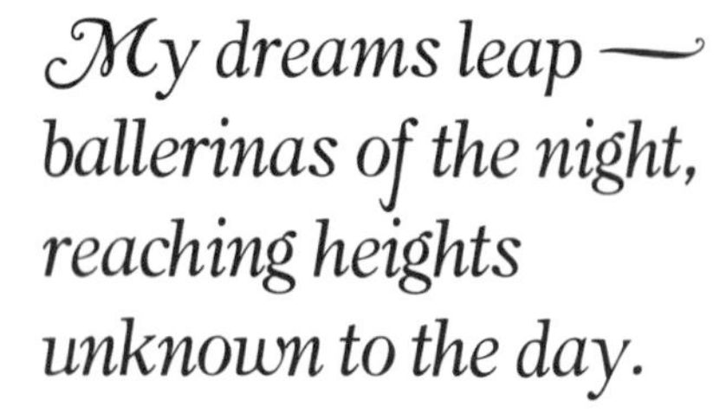

My dreams leap —
ballerinas of the night,
reaching heights
unknown to the day.

Terri Guillemets

Your life is a reflection of how you sleep, and how you sleep is a reflection of your life.

Dr Rafael Pelayo

Sleeping is no mean art: for its sake one must stay awake all day.

Friedrich Nietzsche

A–Z
OF DREAM
INTERPRETATION

COMMON IMAGES IN DREAMS

Research shows that a few images continually crop up in dreams. It is worth looking closely at their meaning or symbolism, because the themes they reveal can often make interpretation simpler. To help with this, the final section of this book contains an alphabetical list of the most common elements and images that occur in dreams, and what they mean. The interpretations come from ancient sources as well as from folklore and psychoanalytic thought.

Interestingly, some images have been found to be common across many different cultures. It is possible that these are so potent because they are among the first impressions that we have as babies, or perhaps there is actually an innate 'commonality of awareness' present in every human being.

The more we learn to interpret our dreams, the more creative and wide-ranging we can become in our search for solutions. Within many cultures there developed a group of people who were the 'dreamers of dreams' – shamans, priests and gurus who were capable of interpreting personal dreams but were also able to interpret dreams they had on behalf of the whole community. In the modern-day world, that facility has been almost lost, so on an individual basis we must now rely on the printed word as a substitute for such people, and learn to interpret our own dreams.

This brings us to a point which cannot be stressed too strongly: *you are the best interpreter of your own dreams*. Even with conventional explanations, you will give them your own twist. The way your mind puts the images together is your own 'dialect' in the language of dreams, and while others may speak a little of your dialect, it may not be totally accurate. For this reason, it is a good idea to discuss your dreams with someone else – partly because you may well remember other aspects of the dream which had slipped your mind, and partly because someone else may have a perception of you that you do not have. You may even wish to set up a discussion group among your friends or family where you interpret your dreams in a group setting. Ultimately, however, you must give your own explanations and interpretations.

Note that you should never take your dreams at face value. For example, dreaming of an argument with a friend does not necessarily mean that you will have such an argument; it may simply mean that you do not agree with something they are doing or saying. It may also mean that that a part of you that is similar to your friend – and probably the reason why you get on well together – is at odds with your own drives or ambitions at this particular time. It is for you to decide which interpretation is correct.

ABYSS

An abyss suggests that we recognize within ourselves the so-called bottomless pit or void. There is a fear of losing control, of a loss of identity, or of some type of failure. We must take a risk without knowing what the outcome is going to be.

ALONE

Being single, isolated or lonely in dreams can suggest issues to do with independence. Loneliness can be experienced as a negative state, whereas being alone can be positive. In dreams a feeling can be highlighted in order for us to recognize whether it is positive or negative, and whether we can deal with our own emotional make-up without the help of others. Often being alone in a dream suggests that there is a wholeness or completeness about us which indicates a degree of self-sufficiency.

ARCH

Passing through an arch or doorway in dreams usually indicates some kind of initiation or rite of passage. We move into a new phase of life, perhaps taking on new responsibilities, learning new skills and meeting new people. There may be some kind of test, but the way is not barred to us: we simply are required to make the effort.

ATTACK

The interpretation of the dream will depend on whether the dreamer is being attacked or is the aggressor. Being attacked in a dream indicates a fear of being under threat from external events or internal emotions. Impulses or ideas which the dreamer does not fully understand force the dreamer into taking a defensive position. If the dreamer is the attacker, they need a more positive form of self-expression.

BALLOON

A balloon is a symbol for joy, and in dreams it may introduce a note of fun amid seriousness. It may often make us aware of our 'humanness', but also our search for the spiritual or more free-spirited side of our personalities, often a feeling of 'light-spirited' joy, or indeed the spirit rising. Very often it is also the colour of balloons in our dreams which can be important.

BEACH

The sea usually suggests emotion, so in dreams to be on a beach shows our awareness of the boundary between emotion and reality, our ability to be in touch with the elements. Depending on our actions and state of mind in the dream, dreaming of a beach usually means relaxation and creativity.

BOOK

Our search for knowledge and the ability to learn from other

people's experience and opinions is symbolized in dreams by books and libraries. To dream of old books represents inherited wisdom and spiritual awareness – sacred ones, such as the Bible or Koran, signify hidden or sacred knowledge. To dream of account books indicates the need or ability to look after our own resources.

BRIDGE

A bridge in a dream signifies the emotional connection between the dreamer and other people or various parts of his life. It is one of the most commonly found images in dreams and almost invariably indicates the crossing from one phase of life to another, some kind of rite of passage, and for this reason it can sometimes indicate death. The bridge may be depicted as weak or strong, sturdy or otherwise, which gives an indication of the strength of connection necessary to make changes in the dreamer's life.

CAGE

The cage normally represents some form of trap or jail. To dream of caging a wild animal alerts us to our need to restrain our wilder instincts. To dream that we are in a cage indicates a sense of frustration and perhaps of being trapped by the past. We are being warned that we are enforcing too much restraint on our hidden abilities. We could be allowing others to hold us back in some way.

CANDLE

To dream of candles indicates that we are trying to clarify something that we do not understand. Candles on a birthday cake can therefore indicate that we are marking a transition from the old to the new. Lighting a candle represents using courage and fortitude or asking for something that we need. Psychologically candles can represent knowledge or wisdom that has not fully crystallized. They can also represent our control of personal magic.

On another level, candles suggest illumination, wisdom, strength and beauty.

CLIFF

To be on the edge of a cliff in a dream indicates the dreamer is facing danger. It shows the need to make a decision as to how to deal with a situation, and possibly be open to taking a risk. We are often facing the unknown. There may be a step we need to take which will psychologically put us either on edge or on the edge in such a way that we must overcome our own fears in order to proceed through our own limitations.

CLOCK

When a clock appears in a dream, we are being alerted to the passage of time. We may need to pay more attention to our own sense of timing or duty, or may need to recognize that there is a sense of urgency in what we are doing. The clock hands in a dream may be indicating those numbers that are important to us. If an alarm clock rings, we are being warned of danger.

DANGER

A dangerous situation in dreams will usually reflect in a graphic, rather exaggerated form the anxieties and dilemmas of everyday life. Dreams can frequently highlight a danger or insecurity in symbolic form, such as conflict, fire or flood. Often such a dream contains a warning of inappropriate action which may be harmful to ourselves or others. Dreaming of oneself in a dangerous or precarious position can also indicate a spiritual insecurity.

DEATH

Death is a stage of transition from an awareness of the physical to the more spiritual side of one's nature. To dream of death, particularly one's own, usually heralds some major change in life, the death perhaps of an old outdated way of being, necessitating a move into the unknown. Dreams of death often occur during those periods in life which were formerly handled by ceremonies and rites of passage, such as puberty to adulthood, maturity to old age.

Death in a dream indicates a challenge which must be confronted. We need to adjust our approach to life and to accept that there can be a new beginning if we have courage.

DOLL

A doll depicts how the dreamer felt as a child, a need for comfort or the reappraisal of childhood experiences which we have forgotten. Only 'coming alive' when played with, a doll may also express some undeveloped part of the dreamer's personality.

DOOR

A door in a dream expresses the idea of a movement between two states of being. It can gain us entry into a new phase of life, such as puberty or middle age. There may be opportunities available to us about which we must make deliberate decisions. If the door in the dream is shut or difficult to open, it indicates that we are creating obstacles for ourselves, whereas if the door is open, we can have the confidence to move forward.

EATING

Being eaten in a dream suggests being attacked by our own – or possibly other people's – emotions and fears. Being eaten by a wild animal shows the likelihood of us being consumed by our more basic, carnal nature or by our internal drives. Hunger is a basic drive, and only once such a drive is satisfied can we move forward to satisfying our more aesthetic needs. To be eating in a dream shows that we are attempting to satisfy our needs or hunger. To refuse food suggests a rejection of growth and the opportunity to change.

ELECTRICITY

Electricity symbolizes power, and it will depend on the context of the dream which aspect of our energy is being highlighted. To dream of electrical wires is to be aware of the dreamer's capability, which may have had to remain hidden for a time. Dreaming of switches is to be aware of the ability to control. To receive an electric shock suggests that we are not protecting ourselves from danger, and need to be more aware.

ESCAPE

Escape suggests our need for spiritual freedom, of attempting to move beyond, or to avoid, difficult feelings. Many anxiety dreams have an element in them of the need to escape, either the situation itself, or something that is threatening us. We may also be trying to escape from something we know we must tackle, such as a responsibility or duty.

EXAMS

Dreaming of taking or being barred from examinations is a fairly typical anxiety dream which has a great deal to do with the standards we set ourselves, and our need for achievement. We have a need to be accepted for what we can do, so some of the occasions which first give us anxiety as children are used by the dreaming self to symbolize other such occasions. Being examined by a doctor or an alien may be in the first place alerting us to concerns over health, though this need not necessarily be physical, and in the second our own need to come to terms with our sense of our own body.

FALLING

The sensation of falling in dreams may be interpreted as the need to be grounded, to take care within a known situation. Equally we may be harmed by being too pedestrian. Falling has also come to be interpreted as sexual surrender and as moral failure – not being as one should. We may not feel that we are properly in control of our lives.

FEATHER

Feathers in a dream could denote softness and lightness, perhaps a more gentle approach to a situation. We may need to look at the truth within the particular situation and to recognize that we need to be calmer in what we are doing. Feathers often represent flight to other parts of the self, and because of their connection with the wind and the air, can represent the more spiritual side of ourselves. To see feathers in a dream perhaps means that we have to complete an action before allowing ourselves to rest.

FLYING

Conventionally, to dream of flying is to do with sex and sexuality, but it would probably be more accurate to look at it in terms of lack of inhibition and freedom. We are releasing ourselves from limitations that we may impose on ourselves. To be flying upwards is to be moving towards a more spiritual appreciation of our lives, while to be flying downwards is to be making an attempt to understand the subconscious and all that entails.

FRIEND

A friend appearing in our dreams can signify one of two things. Firstly, we need to look at our relationship with that particular person and secondly, we need to decide what that friend represents for us (for instance, security, support and love). Often friends highlight a particular part of our own personality that we need to look at, and perhaps understand or come to terms with, in a different way.

GAMES

Playing any game in our dream indicates that we are taking note of how we play the game of life. If we are playing well, we may take it that we are coping well with in life. If we are playing badly, we may need to reassess our abilities and identify the skills we need to improve in order to do better. Specific games such as football, baseball, rugby and cricket, which are team games, represent for many the strong ability to identify with a 'tribe' or a group of people. Games that require the power of thought and strategy give some idea of how we should be taking a situation forward.

GLASS

Glass is a barrier, but it is transparent and therefore allows us to see that which we cannot reach. If we dream of breaking glass, we are probably ready to break free from emotional ties and enter a new phase in our lives. Any barriers that we or others put up can be dealt with successfully. Glass also signifies the barrier of death.

GOBLET

In dreams, the goblet represents the feminine, receptive principle and our ability to achieve enjoyment in different ways. We may be able to make a celebration out of something that is quite ordinary. To be drinking from a goblet indicates allowing ourselves the freedom to enjoy life to the full. To dream of a set of goblets indicates several different ways in which we can make our lives enjoyable and fun.

GOLD

Gold signifies the best, most valuable aspects of ourselves. Finding gold indicates that we can discover those characteristics in ourselves or others. Burying gold shows that we are trying to hide something. Gold in dreams can also represent the sacred, dedicated side of ourselves. We can recognize incorruptibility and wisdom, love and patience. In this context it seldom stands for material wealth, being more the spiritual assets that one has.

HILL

To be on top of a hill indicates that we are aware of our own expanded vision. We have worked hard to achieve something and are able to survey and assess the results of what we have done. To be climbing a hill in the company of others often indicates that we have a common goal – that a journey we thought was ours alone is actually not – and we can use their knowledge to help us. To dream that we are going downhill indicates that we are feeling as if circumstances are pushing us in a certain direction.

HOLIDAY

To be on holiday in a dream indicates a sense of relaxation and of satisfying one's own needs without having to take care of others. It could also, however, be a warning that it is time to take a break from everyday life.

HOME

The home, and particularly the parental home, can stand for shelter, warmth and nourishment. To dream of being at home signifies a return to the standards we learnt as a child. The home can also represent sanctuary, a place where we can be ourselves without fear of reprisal.

HURRICANE

When we experience a hurricane in a dream, we are sensing the force of an element in our lives that is beyond our control. A hurricane can also be symbolic of our passion – we may need to decide whether we can control it – with the consequences for others being of importance.

ILLNESS

Dreaming of illness may alert us to the fact that all is not well either with ourselves or our environment. The nature of the illness may give some indication as to what is amiss, or it may highlight what needs to be done in order to make a situation improve.

IMMOBILITY

To be made immobile in a dream is to suggest that either the energy has run out of a particular situation, or that there is nowhere else to go. It can also mean that we need to take 'time out' to consider our next move.

INVISIBLE

If we are invisible in a dream, this denotes that there is something we want to put behind us and forget. If something is invisible,

then it shows we just need to recognize the presence of something without having to look at it too closely to begin with.

ISLAND

Dreaming of an island signifies loneliness. An island can also represent safety in that, by isolating ourselves, we are not subject to external demands. Occasionally we all need to recharge our batteries, and to dream of an island can help or warn us to do this, which will in turn help us to function better. On another plane, an island can signify a retreat – somewhere that is cut off from the world – which will allow us to contemplate our inner self.

JAR

In old-style symbolism, a jar or any kind of hollow container represents womanhood. For a woman it can represent her ability to be a mother, and in a man it can represent the principle of 'mothering'. On a slightly more esoteric note, a jar can suggest the more sensitive side of our nature, so being jarred or shaken up represents being hurt by what is happening. If the jar is broken, one has received some deep hurt.

JUDGE

Often when we are attempting to stabilise two different states or ways of being, the figure of justice or balance can appear within a dream. This is to warn us that we may need to use both the physical and spiritual aspects of ourselves successfully. Since justice is usually to do with the correct way to do things according to group belief, we may feel that there is the need to conform with others – that we are doing, or are about to do, something which goes against the grain.

JUMPING

The act of jumping can be somewhat ambiguous in a dream. Repetitive movement usually suggests the need to look at what we are doing and perhaps to express ourselves in a different way. Jumping up can indicate reaching for something that is above us, beyond our reach and requires effort to achieve, while jumping down can mean exploring the unconscious or those parts of ourselves which we have not yet examined. Jumping up and down can indicate frustration or joy.

JUNGLE

A jungle can often represent chaos. This chaos can be either positive or negative, depending on other elements in the dream, and may suggest some kind of obstacle that has to be passed through in order to reach a new state of understanding. Being trapped in a jungle suggests that we may be trapped by negative and frightening feelings from the unconscious, although having come through a jungle would indicate that we have passed through and overcome aspects of our lives which we have previously found difficult.

KEYS

Keys often appear in dreams, and have obvious significance in that they lock or unlock that which needs opening or closing. This may be one's potential or perhaps old memories, experiences or emotions. For instance, if the key opens a door, something will be revealed – usually to our advantage, whereas if it locks the door, we are trying to shut something away, perhaps the past or situations we do not wish to handle. To dream of a bunch of keys suggests the need to 'open up' the whole of our personalities to new experiences. Peering through a keyhole shows that our vision and understanding is restricted in some way, or that we are being excluded from activity. Being unable to fit a key into a keyhole indicates inappropriate behaviour.

KILLING

Killing is an extreme answer to a problem. It indicates the violent ending to a predicament. Killing someone in a dream is attempting to be rid of the power they have over us. Dreaming of being killed

suggests that factors with which the dreamer is dealing are making them, or a part of them, ineffective in everyday life.

KNEELING

Kneeling usually suggests submission or sometimes supplication. Initially, kneeling represented giving someone or something status in our lives – that is, putting ourselves on a lower level. In dreams, this is the most frequent explanation. If kneeling is simply a way of being in contact with the earth, it will indicate the need to be in contact with the basic aspects of life.

KNOCKING

Hearing knocking in a dream is often a warning of some kind of difficulty. Our attention needs to be refocused on the matter in hand. For example, if in a dream we are knocking on a door, it may be that we are wanting some attention or approval. We may be feeling excluded from a particular situation or event. It could also suggest that we are trying to be with someone, but do not feel particularly confident of our right to be there.

LADDER

In dreams, the ladder often represents our ability to move from one phase of existence to another, and denotes how secure we feel in moving from one situation to another. Such a dream may occur during career changes and can signify promotion. Probably the most well-known ladder dream is the 'Jacob's Ladder' one recounted in the Bible. This signifies the transition between earth and heaven, and in this context the ladder shows the ability to move from the physical realms of existence into an awareness of the spiritual dimension in life. In spiritual development, such a dream is fairly commonplace.

LAMENESS

A loss of confidence and strength suggests that part of our personality is not functioning correctly. This will often manifest in dreams as lameness. As we become more proficient in interpretation, lameness on the left side will show difficulty with the softer sensitive feminine, while on the right it will suggest

problems with the masculine assertive side of the personality. In mythological terms, lameness is taken to represent the imperfections of the physical realms which are a necessary part of existence.

LATE

Being aware of being late in a dream suggests that we are not totally in control of situations around us. Psychologically, such a dream represents the search for perfection and the feeling that we have or maybe will let someone down. If someone else is late, we are aware that there is a lack of communication.

LIGHT

Any kind of light in a dream usually means illumination. It is much to do with confidence. In dreams, it is often the quality of the light which is important. For instance, a bright light suggests intuition, while a dim light might suggest the potential for sickness. To feel lighter signifies feeling better about ourselves.

MAP

A map in dreams can represent the help we need in our quest to find the way forward. It often indicates the clarification of the direction we should be taking in life. It is worth remembering that we need to read the map ourselves, and therefore we are our own guides. Not being able to read a map might therefore indicate confusion, while knowing we need a map but not having one might suggest a lack of information. An old map shows we perhaps need to look at past experiences if something is troubling us.

MAZE

A maze often represents a confusion of ideas and feelings. Psychologically, the maze in a dream may suggest the variety of opinions and authoritative beliefs that we come up against in our ordinary, everyday world, and which may represent blocks to progress. There are conflicting drives and assumptions, and we often discover that in attempting to find our way through the maze we have learnt something about our own courage, our own ability to

meet problems. Often there is the apparently irrational fear and doubt that arises from not being able to find our way in and out of the maze. This can allow us to release feelings of self-doubt and fear through dreams.

MIRROR

The mirror suggests self-realization backed up by wisdom. Dreaming of a mirror suggests concern over one's self-image. We are worried about what others think of us, and need self-examination or reflection in order to function correctly. There may be some anxiety over ageing or health. By association, it may be that our behaviour needs adjusting.

MUSIC

Music in dreams can equally represent a sensuous and sensual experience. Musical instruments can symbolize the way we communicate with others. For instance, wind instruments tend to suggest the intellect. Percussion instruments suggest the basic rhythm of life.

NAKED

Dreaming of being naked has various connotations, but most revolve around self-image or self-expression and the need to be seen for what we are, not what is projected. Nudity is also linked with innocence and with that the desire to be open and honest. This could tie in with the need for a new start; in effect – and bearing in mind we are born naked – a rebirth.

NEW

When, during a dream, a sense of 'newness' is felt, it usually represents new beginnings, new ways of progressing, or possibly even new relationships. It is also a time to look at how we can learn anew, or maybe even relearn old rules and evaluate from there.

NIGHT

Night is usually the time we can gather strength and relieve ourselves of the day's torment. The antithesis is one of fear and restlessness. We must rid ourselves of the latter symbolism in

order to use the night as a forerunner to a 'new day' and a fresh approach. It must also be said that night can symbolize death, so we must look closely at the dream to determine whether this is so, and if it is, what we can do about it. It does not have to be negative: it could be, for example, the death of a situation or relationship that will ultimately move us on.

NUMBERS

When numbers are brought into focus in dreams, they can have a personal and/or a symbolic significance. Often a number will turn up which has personal meaning, such as a relevant date, or the number of a house in which we may have lived. Our minds will retain the significance of the number, even though we do not always consciously remember it ourselves. It is also worth noting that numbers are infinite, and that mathematics is the link between humanity and science.

OASIS

All around the world an oasis is viewed as a place of sanctuary, where we may live forever in peace and contentment while receiving emotional invigoration. Our worries and anxieties should cast no shadow, until they eventually fade away into a distant blur. We then feel fully refreshed and can come together, step out, and roll with whatever life throws at us.

OBSTACLE

In dreams as in wakefulness, obstacles, whether the physical or emotional kind, have to be scaled, yet that is generally easier said than done. However, how we overcome obstacles in a dream is often a pointer to how we can handle such things as self-doubt and indecision in real life.

ORCHARD

An orchard signifies our ability to look after our interests. If the orchard is showing flowers, then we have what is required to be a

success. If it is a fruit orchard, then we are being reassured that the work we are doing will come to fruition. Another branch of orchard symbolism is fertility; indeed, any collection of trees can signify fertility, but an orchard suggests a more orderly way of going about things.

ORNAMENT

Ornaments, whether religious or secular, become part of our personal space, though the original intent was to enhance that space. In dreams, it is this symbolism which is important. It may be, for instance, within a relationship that we feel under-valued and somewhat taken for granted, like an ornament. If so, we should act quickly to rectify the situation. On the other hand, it may be that we have something of meaning and worth that we wish to elevate to a better position. This of itself signifies that we need to use our own time and space more constructively in order to bring greater success.

PARALYSIS

When paralysis is felt in a dream, we are experiencing some kind of fear or suppression. Feelings that are emotionally based are felt as paralysis; this is to highlight the physical effect those feelings can have. The imagination can play tricks on us, and when we experience as real some kind of reaction we would not normally allow ourselves, it comes across as paralysis.

PARTY

When we dream we are attending a party, we are alerted to our social skills – or lack of them. In waking life we may be shy and dislike such gatherings, but in dreams, if we are coping with the groups involved, we have a greater awareness of our own belonging. On a more obvious level, we may need a celebration of some sort.

PET

A pet appearing in a dream means we are linking in with our natural desire to give and receive love. We may need to 'look after' someone (or something), possibly more vulnerable than us.

PUPPET

When a puppet appears in a dream, there is often a sense of being able to manipulate circumstances or people around us. If someone else is working the puppet, we may feel that it is we who are being manipulated. If the puppet is manipulating us, then we need to be aware of some sort of official difficulty. We may also sense that, as the puppet, we are part of something bigger.

QUEST

The 'hero's quest' is an archetypal image that can appear in many guises in dreams. To be searching for something usually signifies that we are aware that we must undertake a frightening task in order to progress. Many fairy stories and mythological tales have as their main theme the search for something magical. Such themes can be translated into dreams on a personal level.

QUESTION

To be asking questions in a dream indicates a degree of self-doubt. To have someone asking the dreamer questions shows us we are aware that we have some knowledge to share. If the question cannot be answered, the dreamer may need to seek the answer themselves in waking life. If we have a question in waking life that needs answering, by keeping it in mind before going to sleep we may often find the answer through dreams.

QUICKSAND

Quicksand signifies a lack of security, possibly in all aspects of our life. To find ourselves trapped in quicksand suggests that we have been put in a difficult situation that is not necessarily of our own making.

QUILT

To dream of a quilt or duvet is to identify our need for security, warmth, care and love. A particular quilt may have a special significance. For instance, a childhood quilt in an adult dream would suggest the need for some kind of reassurance.

RAFT

On an emotional level, a raft represents a certain kind of safety and stability during a difficult time. It will give us the required security, but in time we will need to have a more solid foundation on which to make the necessary transition.

RAILWAY

Dreaming of railways indicates that we have some tiny indecision on our mind. That is, we are wondering if, in life, we are on the right track and if not, which way to go. If, in the dream, we can see only one track, then there may be only one way to go. If we can see more than one way, then we have more opportunities and need to take more time choosing our way ahead.

READING

Reading a book indicates that we are actively seeking knowledge or information. Also, to be aware that we are reading a novel is to

begin to understand our own need for fantasy. A psychic reading often uses many basic dream images. To dream of having such a reading suggests a need to understand ourselves on a deeper level. Reading, or being in a library, appears in dreams as a form of spiritual realization.

RUNNING

When running occurs in a dream, we need to establish the time and place as this will have a bearing on the symbolism. As an example, one of the most common 'running' dreams is that of actually not being able to run away from somebody; this indicates fear and an inability to do something – a common element in anxiety dreams.

SCHOOL

In situations where we are learning new abilities or skills, the image of a school, or 'school of life', will often appear in dreams. However, we may also be learning about the nature of people and relationships. Alternatively, a school will often appear at a time when we are attempting to get rid of antiquated ideas and concepts.

SEARCHING

To be searching in a dream is to be attempting to find a solution to a problem. If we are searching for someone, we may be aware of our loneliness. If we are searching for something, then there is something we want or need that we have yet to find. In another area, a move towards enlightenment often stems from a feeling of searching for something.

STEPS

Steps in dreams almost always suggest the effort we need to put in to succeed. Going up steps suggests trying to make things better, whereas going down means going either into the past or the subconscious. Either way, there is a change in awareness necessary.

SWIMMING

In dreams, swimming in water is symbolic of the emotions. However, there are different variations; to be swimming upstream would indicate that the dreamer is going against their own nature. Swimming in clear water indicates being cleansed, whereas dark water could symbolize the possibility of depression.

TEETH

Teeth are said to stand for aggressive sexuality. Teeth falling or coming out easily means we are going through some form of transition – for example, from childhood to maturity, or from maturity to old age and helplessness. If one is anxious about teeth dropping out, this suggests a fear of getting old and undesirable, or an anxiety about maturing. In a woman's dream, if the teeth are swallowed this can signify pregnancy.

TRANSFORMATION

Dreams where changes occur and things are transformed into something else suggest a shift in awareness and freedom of thought. A landscape may change from dark to light (negativity to positivity); a person may change from masculine to feminine; or one image may change into another. Once the dreamer understands the change is for the better, they are able to accomplish changes in their own life.

TRAP

To be in a trap in a dream signifies that we feel we are trapped by outside circumstances. To be aware of trapping something or someone is attempting to hold onto them. When we feel trapped in dreams, we are not usually able to break free from old patterns of thought and behaviour – we may need outside help. On another plane, it may suggest that we are holding ourselves back.

TUNNEL

A tunnel in a dream represents the need to explore our own unconscious, and those things we have left untouched. A tunnel can also symbolize the birth canal and therefore the process of birth. If there is a light at the end of the tunnel, it indicates we are reaching the final stages of our exploration. If something is blocking the tunnel, some past fear or experience is stopping us from progressing. In another sense, the image of a tunnel helps us to escape from the unconscious into the light, and also to go down into the depths.

UMBRELLA

As we mature, we need to develop certain coping skills. In dreams, these can be seen as a protective covering, often seen as the shelter and sanctuary of an umbrella. It is this symbolism that comes across in dreams. Often in a work situation the large corporation acts as an umbrella and we need to work under someone else's teaching. This notion can often be perceived in dreams as an umbrella.

UNDERGROUND

The subconscious or unconscious is often perceived as a cave or place underground. Dreams give us opportunities to explore our own hidden depths. To dream of being underground will often allow us to come to terms with that side in a very easy way. To dream of being on the underground or subway usually signifies the journeys we are prepared (or forced) to take towards understanding ourselves.

UNICORN

When a unicorn appears in a dream, we are linking with the innocent, pure part of ourselves. This is the instinctive, receptive feminine principle. There is a story that unicorns missed being taken into Noah's Ark because they were too busy playing. We need to be mindful of what is going on in the real world if we are to survive. The unicorn can also signify that rarest of qualities – unconditional love.

UNIVERSITY

Dreaming of being in a university highlights our own individual potential and learning ability. Since a university is a place of 'higher' learning, we are being made aware of the breadth of experience and increase in knowledge available to us. We need to move away from the mundane and ordinary into specific areas of knowledge and awareness.

VASE

As a holder of beautiful things, any receptacle – such as a vase, water pot, pitcher or urn – tends to represent the feminine within a dream, the accepting and receptive nature of the feminine, intuitive side. Such an object can also signify the Great Mother and hence, by association, creativity.

VICTORY

The victory dream scenario may be a conflict between two aspects of ourselves, or require us to overcome some difficulty. This can often be recognized as a difficulty we have created for ourselves, and which by achieving victory gives us confidence in ourselves.

VIOLENCE

Any violence in dreams is a reflection of our own inner feeling, sometimes about ourselves, sometimes about the situations

around us. Often the type of violence is worthy of notice if we are fully to understand ourselves. Violence in dreams can arise because we are unable to express our aggression appropriately in everyday life.

VOLCANO

An erupting volcano usually signifies that we are not in control of a situation or of our emotions – of which there may be a hurtful release. If the lava is more prominent, feelings will run very deep. If the lava has cooled, there has been a deep passion which has now cooled off. If the explosiveness is more noticeable, anger may be more prominent. To dream of a volcano being extinct can indicate either that we have 'killed off' our passions, or that a difficult situation has come to an end.

WAITING

To be waiting for somebody or something in a dream implies a need to recognize the importance of patience. We must wait for the passage of time. We may be looking to other people or outside circumstances to help us move forward or make decisions. If *we* are impatient, it may be that our expectations are too high.

WALKING

In a dream, walking indicates the way in which we should be moving forward, a journey of exploration. To be walking purposefully suggests we know where we are going. To be wandering aimlessly suggests we need to create goals for ourselves. To take pleasure in the act of walking is to return to the innocence of the child, or to obtain relief from stress. To be using a walking stick is to recognize our need for support and assistance.

WATER

Water is usually taken in dreams to symbolize all that is emotional and feminine. It can also stand for the dreamer's potential and their ability to create a new life in response to their own inner urgings. Water appears so often in dreams as an image, with so many different meanings, that it is possible only to suggest some probable ones. Thus, being immersed in water can suggest pregnancy and birth. Flowing water signifies peace and comfort, while rushing water can indicate passion.

WRITING

Writing gives substance to our thoughts and allows us to communicate when spoken words are inadequate. In dreams we may learn how to communicate with ourselves in differing ways. To dream of writing is an attempt to communicate information that one has. Sometimes the instrument we are writing with is important. For instance, a pencil would suggest that the information is less permanent than with a pen.

X

If the letter X appears in a dream, we are usually 'marking the spot'. This can also represent an error or something that we particularly need to note. If a cross appears in the shape of an X, this usually represents the idea of sacrifice or perhaps of torture.

YIN-YANG

The yin-yang symbol signifies a state of dynamic potential. In dreams it indicates the balance between the instinctive, intuitive nature of the feminine and the active, rational nature of the masculine, and our need to establish a balance between the two.

ZIP

Psychologically, we are capable of being either open or closed to our friends and family. Often a zip in a dream can highlight this. A stuck zip suggests a difficulty in keeping our dignity in an awkward situation.

ZOO

Dreaming of being in a zoo suggests the need to understand some of our natural urges and instincts. There may be an urge to return to simpler, more basic modes of behaviour. We perhaps need to be more objective in our appraisal than subjective.

INDEX

S

T

U

V

W

Y